PRAISE FOR
A ROCK IN THE CLOUDS

This is a firsthand and intimate retrospective centered around an absolutely harrowing and deadly plane crash during the height of the Vietnam War more than a half century ago. But it is also an autobiography filled with memorable stories of brotherhood, faith, and love among soldiers far from home and those who cared for them.

Beautifully written and woven from personal recollections of a tragic era in American history, it includes both the highs and lows of grievous injury, loss, and recovery, but also—and more profoundly—of devotion, service, character, redemption, and especially the lasting bonds of family and friendship.

Although so many from that era are now gone, this book tells a timeless story that matters still. I know that it will endure in my heart—and, I hope, in our collective national memory—always.

—**Robert W. Ray**, Former Whitewater Independent Counsel

A gripping account of a pivotal event in Joseph Tedeschi's distinguished life and career. From a boyhood in the mill town of Natick in Rhode Island to the hallowed halls of West Point, the author weaves his life's story around a fateful crash into a monsoon-obscured mountain at An Khe during the Vietnam War. One of the survivors, the author has pieced together what happened on that fateful day in 1966. As Tedeschi writes, "A war never ends until the last story is written." At the age of eighty-seven, retired colonel Joseph Tedeschi has added his voice to the stories told by veterans of this war. It is worthy of your read.

—**James Ballard**, Vietnam War Medic, Author of
Poisoned Jungle and *Mekong Delta Blues*

A Rock in the Clouds compellingly tells of the author's quest for the answer to a question many have struggled with—"Why me?" On 4 October 1966, a Caribou aircraft plowed into the side of Hong Cong Mountain in Vietnam. While thirteen soldiers died, the author survived. For fifty-five years the author's agonizing struggle to find a meaningful answer to his existential question led to intense reflection on his life experiences. In a genuinely moving yet entertaining manner, he shares varied stories of his rich life. The underlying theme is the importance that family and faith played in helping him through the emotional turmoil he experienced. His faith was a powerful source of strength through his long rehabilitation and quest for answers. His faith answered his question eighty years ago, and it suddenly became crystal clear that God wanted him to be able to continue to "Know, love, and serve Him."

An inspirational read which can result in thinking as the author does, "Every day is Christmas!"

—**David E. Schorr**, Colonel US Army (Ret.),
West Point Class of '57

Thank God the author survived a horrific plane crash in Vietnam to tell his story. His details of the crash put the reader at the scene. He recounts the recovery from his injuries and the years leading up to the time when he can now relay his experiences to all of us. This book vividly describes one of many hellacious situations and the aftereffects suffered by our troops who fought the war in Vietnam. Thanks to Joseph Tedeschi for sharing his story and for his dedicated service to our country.

—**George W. Kohn**, Colonel US Air Force (Ret.),
Award-Winning Author of *Vector to Destiny:
Journey of a Vietnam F-4 Fighter Pilot*

Joe Tedeschi describes surviving a plane crash into a mountain in Vietnam which severely injured him. His book describes the ordeal and how it continues to shape his life half a century later with eloquence, depth, and wisdom. Indeed, he has created a priceless story of heroism, love, resilience, patriotism, and faith which will help his readers, his kids, and his grandkids (and their kids and grandkids) fashion their own "lives well lived" as they move forward.

—**Bill McCusker**, Founder of Fathers & Families, Inc.

A soldier's story is one of service, sacrifice, and camaraderie. From my grandfather's World War II letters to my own experiences overseas, it is easy to infer that times change, but soldiers for the most part never do. Col. Tedeschi captures that essence as he tells a horrific story of his tragic accident in Vietnam that he survived only by the sheer grace of God.

His tale begins with his upbringing, paying great tribute to those who helped mentor him into the man he became. The gravity of the plane crash that is the genesis for Col. Tedeschi's book cannot be overstated, but ironically, living was the "easy" part. The perseverance, love, and dedication that he displayed throughout his recovery is remarkable and a great read.

I highly recommend *A Rock in the Clouds* to military enthusiasts, service members, veterans, and their families. Additionally, I recommend it for anyone just trying to gain perspective in their life. After Col. Tedeschi's remarkable survival and recovery, it's easy to understand why he believes every day is like Christmas. Through his words, though, I believe we could all gain some appreciation of our own lives.

—**Benjamin Warner**, Author of *20 Year Letter:*
An Afghanistan Chronicle

A Rock in the Clouds: A Life Revisited

by Col. Joseph R. Tedeschi, US Army (Ret.)

ISBN 978-1-64663-480-4

Published by

köehlerbooks™

3705 Shore Drive
Virginia Beach, VA 23455
800-435-4811
www.koehlerbooks.com

COL. JOSEPH R. TEDESCHI
US ARMY (RET.)

A ROCK

IN THE

CLOUDS

A Life Revisited

VIRGINIA BEACH
CAPE CHARLES

DEDICATION

*To the honored memory of all who died or were injured
in the crash of "Critter 23" and their families*

*To Sue, Susanne, and Marly and all my family
for your precious love and support*

To Bob and Peggy Ray

*To My Mother, My Confidence
Mater Mea, Fiducia Mea*

A life that is not reflected upon isn't worth living. It belongs to the essence of being human that we contemplate our life, think about it, discuss it, evaluate it, and form opinions about it. Half of living is reflecting on what is being lived.

Henri Nouwen

CONTENTS

Part 3: A Life Examined

FOREWORD

THERE IS A GRIM, descriptive saying among pilots and old flying hands that when an aircraft is flying blind through thick clouds and fog and the aircraft collides with an object thus hidden, it has found a "rock in the clouds." The chances of this happening today, especially in commercial aviation, are quite slim with the advent of better aircraft flight control procedures and radar warning devices.

However, in the history of military aviation, there are a number of tragic incidents where this has happened—some quite sensational. For example, the B-25 bomber that flew into the Empire State Building in 1944 when all Manhattan was engulfed in low hanging clouds. Edward Doylerush documented numerous military high-ground crashes in the mountains of South Wales during World War II in his 2008 book, *Rocks in the Clouds*. Also, a *New Yorker* magazine article documented the complexity of identifying human remains, specifically reporting on trying to identify the remains of the crew of a military aircraft that found a "rock in the clouds" while "flying the hump" over the Himalayas during World War II.

This is a story about another military airplane that found a "rock in the clouds" in Vietnam. On 4 October 1966, a C7-A Caribou airplane flying through blinding cloud cover crashed into Hon Cong Mountain near the base camp of the 1st Air Cavalry Division at An Khe. There were thirty-one people aboard the aircraft, an air crew of four along with twenty-seven passengers. Thirteen people died in the crash. I was one of the survivors.

I recall the moments just before the crash. I became aware of the aircraft's descent and the start of landing approach procedures. I kept glancing out the window near me trying to see the airfield or any ground features that might give me a clue as to where we were. However, all I could see were thick clouds—no ground visibility. The aircraft seemed to be going in circles with the pilot making some sharp turns as we descended even further.

I heard the pilot finally lower the gear for landing. With the landing wheels down, our speed was somewhat reduced, but we continued to descend with circular turns. I still could not see the ground through the thick clouds. Suddenly, both engines gave a deafening roar, alerting everyone to the impending danger. The front end of the aircraft pitched violently upward just before we crashed—altering my life completely.

All airplane crashes are tragedies, but under wartime conditions, the resulting chaos is magnified. The tempo of war demands that all the pieces be put together quickly, and the brisk pace of war continues. But for the survivors involved in the crash, the pace of the war suddenly stops, and they have the remainder of their lives to reflect and ponder numerous unanswered questions.

It has taken fifty-five years for me to piece together a more complete account of the crash. The details evolved in bits and pieces over the years and involved many people who helped me. I was able to obtain photos and accounts of the crash from others who survived or who were witnesses on the scene. This information and my own recollections allowed me to develop and document a comprehensive account of the crash details.

As I worked on this account, it began to evolve into much more than just a description of an airplane crash. In the evolution, I began to realize it was becoming a very human story of the people involved and the impact it had on their lives and families after the crash.

Not a day goes by since the crash that I do not reflect on that shattering instant of my life. In a moment of forced reflection as I lay in a hospital bed recovering from my injuries, I solemnly resolved to find some meaning and purpose to what had suddenly happened to me. My immediate resolve that day was a renewed commitment to my family, the sustaining foundation of my life. My family will always provide sufficient meaning and purpose for all things, including surviving the crash. But I needed something more to fully satisfy my resolve. Judeo-Christian principles of faith have informed and sustained me all my life, guiding me where to seek my answers. I began to search out the roots of that faith to find these answers.

My spiritual life since the beginning has been one of continual conversion, and my search forced me to look back at my life both before and after the crash. I began to realize that many of my spiritual life experiences before the crash were part of a path that led me to that fateful day. I was thirty-two years old when the crash occurred, and, writing this at eighty-six, I can look back on a life marked by numerous and various shifts and changes; but at each stage when decision and risk were involved, I was guided by something bigger and outside of myself. I unabashedly thank God for his steadying hand at every turn.

A war never ends until the last story is told. Mine is certainly not the last story to be told of the Vietnam War, but I sincerely hope it will be one of the last.

LOOKING BACK AFTER FIFTY YEARS

Over the years since the crash, I have been compelled to integrate this experience into my outlook on life—and yes, I have my share of "survivor's guilt." My ears perk up every time I hear or read about an airplane crash. I've been forced to ponder, wonder about, consider, think about, reflect upon, come to an understanding, and accept why I survived that crash. I've tried to relate and express these thoughts and feelings in various ways, written and verbal, as the opportunities presented themselves over the years. In 2007 I wrote a fifty-year life summary for the yearbook to commemorate my West Point Class of 1957 Reunion. This mini-autobiography was bracketed between photos showing me as a cadet at West Point and a current photo "as you are" fifty years later. On the following page are the photos followed by what I wrote for the yearbook:

Joseph Raymond (Joe) Tedeschi   **L1/ Artillery-Chemical Corps**
Sue   **Medford N.J**

My Cadet and 50 Years Later photos

When I walked through that sally port, I knew so little about West Point and even less about the Army. Nothing in my Rhode Island upbringing pointed me in this direction. It launched a whole new world for me. The true love of my life, Sue Oebbecke, "joined the Army too" on 20 July 1957. Both our daughters were born Army Brats, Susanne (Hawaii) and Marly (Aberdeen Proving Ground). Career favorites: Army sponsored advanced schooling at Iowa State University, exchange officer with the British Army at their Defence NBC School, several Washington/Pentagon assignments, [and being the] Commander/Director of the Foreign Science and Technology Center in Charlottesville, VA.

In Vietnam, 1966, I experienced one of those life-altering events: I survived as a passenger when the Caribou aircraft flew into the side of Hon Cong Mountain at An Khe. Over the years, I've learned to describe this experience in a shorthand way: Every day is Christmas!

I began a second career for 14 years with General Electric/ Martin Marietta/Lockheed Martin—same job, different bosses, as Program Manager for the Counter Battery Radar (COBRA). I lived this program from its concept, sold it as a package to the governments of France, Germany, and the United Kingdom, and retired in 1999 after the first three prototypes were built. A very satisfying experience.

My latest venture occurred when I entered the diaconate program in the Diocese of Trenton just prior to my second retirement and I was ordained a deacon in 2002. It's been 26 moves since I walked through that sally port, but life seems to have settled down now around Medford, NJ, St. Mary of the Lakes Parish, our condo in Brigantine, our daughters and their great husbands, and our five wonderful grandchildren. Every day is Christmas!

It was a challenge to capture fifty years of my life in the limited space allotted between the two photos. I chose to highlight the plane crash because it was the seminal story of my life during those fifty years, but as I reflected on what I wrote, I realized this mini-autobiography provided a capsule summary of my life and would be useful as an overarching outline for the narrative of my story. Accordingly, I start my story with "when I walked through that sally port."

PART 1
FREE TO SEARCH FOR
SOMETHING GOOD

CHAPTER 1
CONFLICTING MOTIVES

"When I walked through that sally port, I knew so little about West Point and even less about the Army . . ."

THE "SALLY PORT" IS a covered walkway leading into the Central Barracks at West Point. Candidates traditionally enter here for the first time. I really knew very little about the army and West Point prior to entering the academy. I had spent my first year of college at St. Lawrence University. My year in the Army ROTC there gave me some insights, but hardly enough to prepare me for what came next. I was strongly motivated by this opportunity to go to West Point as the solution to all my financial concerns for getting a college education. During Beast Barracks (the first six weeks of new cadet training), I began to realize the price I had to pay to get that education.

Beast Barracks is intended to weed out those without motivation, and I was sorely tested. My initial motivation to get a "free" college education quickly turned to one of pride. They were not going to break me, and I was not going to quit. The alternatives were not very appealing. I could not let the people back home in Natick down. The accolades I heard at the wonderful community send-off dinner still rang in my ears.

Candidates arriving at West Point entering the sally port

I made it through Beast Barracks and the start of the academic year. Plebe year and the Plebe System are legendary, and I found all of it to be true. Throughout my plebe year and all four years at the academy, I was challenged to live and conform to the military ethos and to learn, accept, and believe in the principles underlying the West Point motto: Duty, Honor, Country. By the time I graduated, West Point had become the cornerstone of my future life by preparing me well and pointing me toward a career as an army officer.

My fifty-year look back from 2007 to the time I graduated from West Point on 4 June 1957 really began four years earlier on 7 July 1953 when I walked through that sally port as a West Point candidate. Leading me to this time and place was an earlier life that had been at times uncertain, challenging, and involving some risky adventures. During my first nineteen years, I had been searching and seeking for that "something out there" that would lead to a successful future, but I had no idea what that would be. Entering West Point, I felt that I had found the future I was looking for and had finally arrived at a secure and stable place in my life. However, nothing in my upbringing in Rhode Island from my early years through high school ever suggested a military career.

CHAPTER 2
MY BEGINNINGS

*". . . Nothing in my Rhode Island upbringing pointed me in
this direction . . ."*

I HAVE A STRONG sense of place, and my roots have had a significant impact on my life. I lived the first eighteen years of my life in a dying mill town, Natick, along the banks of the Pawtuxet River in Rhode Island. The history of these mill towns in the Pawtuxet River Valley are noteworthy, and I offer a native son's perspective in Appendix B.

I was named after my paternal grandfather. It was only recently after I obtained a copy of my original birth certificate from Sacred Heart Church, my hometown parish, that I realized I had been baptized the Italian name "Guiseppe" as well. Of course, I have used the anglicized "Joseph" all my life, but to see it as I was baptized on St. Joseph's Day, 19 March 1934, came as quite a surprise to me. My grandfather lived ninety-six years. He was on his death bed when I was leaving for West Point in 1953. Because he died shortly after I entered the academy, I was not able to attend his funeral.

Grandpa Tedeschi and I in 1940 on the occasion of my
First Communion

FAMILY, EARLY LIFE AND EDUCATION

No one had more influence on my early life than my mother. She was my prime parent, first disciplinarian, and inspirational guide. My mother worked the third shift at the Arctic Lace Mills. That meant she had to leave for work around ten at night. I can remember crying and making a fuss every time she had to leave—it became a ritual that she had to lie down with me in bed before she left, trying to comfort me, my older sister too. This must have been in the late 1930s. Times were tough, and I'm sure the money was needed. I can only imagine how tired my mother felt coming home in the early morning after the third shift.

My father was more typical of the Italian men of his generation. They fathered children, worked very hard, but left most of the parenting up to the mother. This is a father I really did not know, and I guess I've always wanted desperately to know. Having lost him when I was seventeen, I have so little to hang on to that was really him. I have spent time trying to reconstruct my father's life from his service record with the navy during World War 1 and from the few letters and cards he wrote during that time.

I began kindergarten at Baker Street School in September 1939, the same month World War II started in Europe. From the time of the Japanese attack on Pearl Harbor on 7 December 1941 to the dropping of the atomic bomb on Hiroshima and Nagasaki in 1945, this world event would paint a backdrop to my life and early school years.

Boys in my kindergarten class - Front: Sammy Parente 4th, Joe 5th;
Back: Turk Petrarca 3rd

The rationing sticks with me, how frightened we were by the shortages of sugar, butter, meat, etc. Air raid drills and the blackouts constantly reminded us of the uncertain times. But surrounding my school days, I also remember the pleasure of seeing the big lilac tree in the corner of the school yard and the smell of lilac blossoms on spring days when the classroom windows were all opened (no air conditioning in those days!).

My sixth-grade teacher, Mrs. Cardin, posted a big map of the world on the blackboard, and we followed the progression of the war by placing pins on the map—especially General MacArthur's island hopping in the Pacific. The island of Luzon in the Philippines especially stuck in my memory—a great way to learn geography. Little did I know that someday I would be there as a result of another war.

For my First Communion, my mother bought me five chicks from the Woolworth's in Arctic, a town south of us. I remember they sold such things in the five and dime stores back then. They had an incubator filled with chicks, and you bought them just like any other purchase!

The purchase was very timely. With the war just starting, we would have our own source of eggs! All was well, but as the chicks grew, it turned out we had two roosters and three hens. It didn't take very long before the dominant rooster got rid of the other rooster. We named the survivor "Blondie" because of the blond streaks he had in his feathers. He clearly ruled the roost—and everything else in sight.

Blondie was very territorial, and he staked out our yard as his turf. This meant *no one* could enter, including the postman, the milkman, and the tenants who were living in our upstairs apartment. Silk was used for making parachutes and was very scarce (nylon stockings were just coming into their own). So, this made Blondie attacking the lady visitors and tearing their stockings quite the travesty.

My brother Mike and I were the only ones Blondie would tolerate and allow to handle him. These transgressions and his threatening the postman really led to his demise. We had him for at least a couple of years, but at some point, my Uncle Mike took his hatchet and did away with him. The cruelest thing: my brother Mike and I did not know it until Blondie showed up at the Sunday dinner table!

By today's standards, my family would have been considered poor, but I certainly was not aware of it. I just didn't see or feel any poverty. I was deceived by all that "poverty" implies. Instead, despite all the trappings of poverty, I was raised in a loving home and nurtured by a caring family, relatives, and community. Many of my memories tie to my involvement with my church. The Sacred Heart Church Parish and the pastor, Father DeAngelis, played a central role in all our lives.

I remember playing baseball behind Sacred Heart Church one summer evening and being called over to the rectory by Father "D." He asked me if I wanted to be an altar boy. I can't remember if I said yes just then or later, but I do remember starting lessons to be an altar boy by going to the rectory on Saturday mornings to learn the responses in Latin.

It was a fairly rigorous schedule. My friend Sammy Parente and I would serve at the weekday 7:30 Mass when it was our turn. This meant getting up very early, walking the mile or so to church, doing our altar boy duties, and then walking to school from there. The Mass was attended mostly by old women wearing black dresses and shawls.

Then there were the Saturday morning weddings. We liked weddings because they occasionally resulted in "tips"! Of course, there were the funerals as well. These were very vivid memories for a young boy to absorb. They rang the church bells at funerals—usually the age of the person being buried. I can remember the big rope that pulled the clapper on the bell, but you didn't get to do that until you were "older."

CHAPTER 3
MAJOR CHANGES

MY LIFE CHANGED RADICALLY between 1950 and 1953. My father began his struggle with cancer in 1950 when I was sixteen and beginning my junior year in high school. I simply did not understand the gravity of his illness at that time. I was so focused on school, sports, and working that I pushed it to the back of my mind.

My brother was working at the Star Super Market in Cranston. As soon as I turned sixteen, Mike was able to get me a part-time job there bagging the groceries and carrying them to people's cars. The base salary was minimal, but "bag boys" were able to get tips. I remember a dime tip was nominal, occasionally a quarter! This was a step up from all my earlier jobs of caddying at Ledgemont Country Club, working as a bus boy for Club 400, or setting pins at the Natick Bowling Alley.

As a collateral duty, I was also employed to stack shelves at the supermarket. I'll never forget the rookie trick they played on me—sending me around the whole store (meat department, produce department, and even the manager's office) looking for a "counter stretcher." I can't remember if I was dismayed or amused when I discovered it was all a big gag!

When news of the Korean War had started in June 1950, I was sitting in the employee's "lounge" (just a table to eat your lunch). Hearing the news, I had no idea what it was all about or even where Korea was on the map!

I played football in the fall, and at the end of the season, my high school, Lockwood, won the state Class C Championship. I was never so proud as when I received the championship jacket the Booster's Club gave to each member of the team that year. I was further honored by being elected captain of the team by my teammates for the following senior year.

It was during this happy, exciting time of my life that my father began suffering his prolonged illness. His initial treatment was a major surgery to remove cancer from his esophagus. At that time, doctors had few options outside of the radical treatment of cutting the cancer out. Chemotherapy and radiation treatment were not common then. I had just obtained my driver's license, and I drove us to Deaconess Hospital in Boston along the old Route 1, a big deal for me—no I-95 yet! My father underwent surgery and then endured a long recovery, but he eventually was well enough to return to his job at Quonset Point Naval Air Station later that year.

I played basketball during the winter of 1950–51 and baseball in the spring. I don't have too many other memories of school my junior year except that I was doing well academically. Sometime during the spring of 1951, I was offered a job as a pot washer at an exclusive, all-girls camp, Teela Wooket, in Roxbury, Vermont. Except for Boy Scout camp, I had never been away from home for more than a week.

SUMMER AWAY FROM HOME

I took the job and set off for Vermont right after school ended. This was a summer of growing experiences. So many memories to record—it would take a whole chapter! I learned so much about "life" from the other members of the kitchen crew which consisted of three cooks—Pat, Sal, and Gino, a former opera singer—our potato peeler John, our head baker, Nick the "Russian," and his assistant Bobby (later drafted and sent to Korea). I rounded out the crew as pot washer.

When the first Sunday came, I told the head cook, Pat, that I would be going to Mass at the little rural church in Roxbury. It came as quite a shock to me when I was told that the kitchen crew did not go to church—we were expected to be in the kitchen working on Sunday mornings. I must have made quite an issue of it, because it took a decision by the head dietitian to permit me to take time off on Sunday mornings to go to church. As I look back on it, I should have realized that just about all the other kitchen crew were also Catholics, but they chose not to go to Mass or were not able to go because of the requirements of their jobs.

I look back in gratitude to all of them for their allowing me to leave each Sunday morning for an hour or so to go to church. I was still serving Mass as an altar boy in my Sacred Heart parish until the time I left for this job. This was my pre-Vatican II mindset—you just did not miss Mass on Sundays. Theirs was a more generous mindset—to allow this teenager to hang on to his beliefs and convictions, even if it meant picking up the slack by his absence.

My summer job of 1951 came to a close about a week early when my sister Theresa, my brother Mike, and a friend came to get me because of my father's serious relapse. How naive I was. I still did not comprehend sickness, cancer, and death. My mind was on the upcoming football season when I was going to be captain of the team. I had received a letter from the coach, Dom DiLuglio, sometime during the summer which really pumped me up. He told me I had to be in good physical shape since I was going to lead the team.

I'll never forget the drive back from Vermont, highlighted by a policeman pulling us over at two in the morning. We were driving my brother-in-law Paul's car since he was away on a navy cruise. Our friend Bobby Carly was driving, and the three siblings were sleeping in the back seat. It took a while to explain who owned the car, who we were, what we were doing, and where we were going at that time of night. Eventually we convinced the policeman, who let us go.

ROUGH PATCH

The next month, September 1951, was a hectic time for me. I started school, practiced football, and seemed to make almost daily visits to my father at the Veteran's Hospital in Providence. We sure kept that old 1940 Chevy busy.

I don't know if I can do justice to the week and day my father died at the end of September. We had stayed at the hospital until very late the night before and left to get some sleep, then returned the next morning. I still thought my father would recover. They let me see him only once, but he was in a coma, and I guess I've tried to erase this memory all my life.

When we arrived early the next morning, I rushed to his room while my mother and siblings, Mike and Theresa, delayed in the waiting room. When I got to his room, it was empty. I asked a nurse where they had moved my father. She did not give me an answer right away, but after some time, she told me my father had died.

I dashed back to the waiting room and told my mother, brother, and sister. What a terrible moment. A doctor came by and told us the details. We left the hospital in pain and agony.

The wake and funeral should have been overwhelming for me, but somehow, I held up better than most of my family. I was still naive, immature, and basically could not take in what was happening. I really didn't know how to act at the time.

I missed one season football game (North Kingston—we won) and was back to school right away. It was probably the best thing for me. I remember crying, but the full impact of my father dying was still beyond me. Maybe I thought the more I occupied myself, the sooner the impact would go away.

Today, I know how badly I was in need of some help and counseling. But things were different then. You didn't fold—you were stoic and "manly." We just didn't have the luxury of counseling then.

For the remainder of that fall, I focused on school and football. We ended the season in a three-way tie for the state Class C Football Championship. The last game of the season was played at East Greenwich, which we had to win in order to claim our share of the three-way tie. We did win, but it was a very tough game. I cried on the bus going back to Lockwood. Somehow, I knew this was the end of something big and fine for me, and I was going to miss it. It clearly was another turning point in my life.

CHAPTER 4
LOOKING AHEAD

If you don't know where you're going, any road will get you there.

Lewis Carroll

AS THE END OF my high school years neared in 1952, I began to assess my plans for the future. I had been brought up and conditioned to believe in the progression model of college and career as the path to success. However, with my father's death, I knew that if I were to go on to college, I would have to do it on my own. I received some help from my football coach and mentor, Dom DiLuglio, who arranged interviews for me at Amherst College and Yale University, but these did not develop into anything, mostly because I would need almost 100% financial assistance to attend one of those schools.

After talking it over with my family, I decided to apply to the University of Rhode Island, which was sufficiently nearby, so I could live at home and still attend classes. Family finances would pay for tuition and books, but campus living was out. My application was accepted, and I was prepared to enter URI in the fall of 1952.

Fortunately, my football coach would not give up on me. He advised me, "Apply to one of the service academies. Better yet, apply to all the service academies, and perhaps one of them will accept you."

The service academies offered what I lacked and desperately

needed: money to go to college. (I learned later you are even paid while attending.) I took his advice, and I can remember my sister and I looking in the dictionary for the correct salutation to address Congressman Fogarty and Senator Pastore from Rhode Island. We sent them identical letters before school ended where I asked for an opportunity to attend one of the service academies at West Point, Annapolis, the Coast Guard Academy, or even the Merchant Marine Academy. I would have applied to the Air Force Academy, but it hadn't been founded yet in 1952!

I did not realize that it takes almost two years to complete an application-testing-acceptance cycle to enter one of the academies. Unless one starts the process during their junior year in high school or early in their senior year, it puts you behind, and you must wait until the following year to catch up with the cycle. I must admit, by the time we sent the letters, I did not have much hope. I resigned myself to the fact that I would be attending URI in the fall.

BACK TO VERMONT AND "POP" SCHOLL

In the meantime, I needed to earn money for college, so I opted to return to my job at Teela-Wooket in Vermont for the summer of 1952—this time as the third cook, an upgrade from pot washer! Yet, once again, someone entered my life who took an interest in me and provided unsolicited help. "Pop" Scholl was the principal of the high school in Watertown, New York. Pop and his wife had taken jobs as counselors at the summer camp for a number of years. Pop had served in the army during World War I and was just a "regular guy."

Over the years at the camp, he became friendly with the kitchen crew, and he soon learned the secret of good eating—find a place at their table in the back room with the cooks! We always ate after the meal had been served to the campers, and somehow, Pop would show up at our table following a meal just for those few "extras" that were served.

During table conversation over a few meals, I told Pop about my background and of my plans to enter URI in the fall. He inquired about my grades and school activities—something you would expect a high school principal to do. For some reason, I happened to have a transcript of my high school records with me, and I showed them to him.

After a week or so went by, Pop took me aside and asked if I would be interested in attending St. Lawrence University in Canton, New York, located just north of Watertown. Pop had two adopted sons going there and thought I might do well in the small college atmosphere.

With my grades and high school record, he felt confident he could get me a late acceptance for the upcoming academic year despite the fact that it was already mid-summer. As a high school principal and with two sons attending there, Pop was very familiar with Dr. Brown, Dean of Students at St. Lawrence University, and thought it might be worth a try.

I clearly was interested. The prospect of attending URI and living at home was not the image I had of "going to college." But I had to tell him that I did not have the finances to attend a small, private university. Pop said he would try to remedy this if I were ready to make a commitment to attend.

At eighteen years old, I had reached a critical decision point in my life that only I could make. I admit I was frightened by the prospect of making the wrong decision. In my short lifetime, I had never traveled outside of the immediate New England states. St. Lawrence University was located in the far north reaches of New York state, right next to the Canadian border. I didn't even know what the place looked like! With some prayers and trepidation, I told Pop to give it a try.

Pop wrote a single letter to Dean Brown with a copy of my high school records—perhaps he even made a few phone calls of which I was not aware. Within a short time, I received a letter from Dean Brown with an offer of an athletic scholarship that paid for most of the tuition along with an opportunity to work in the dormitory kitchen to defray the cost of room and board (a wink to my work experience and recommendation). I accepted the offer, but I knew the finances would still be a problem.

I was very surprised to receive two other letters that summer—one from Congressman Fogarty and one from Senator Pastore. They both acknowledged receipt of my earlier letters that I had sent on the urging of my football coach and asked that I present myself at the West Warwick Post Office that same summer to take a civil service screening exam. I had to ask time off from work, again, and they were gracious enough to grant my request.

I took a train back home, took the exam, and returned to Vermont to finish my summer of work. I still considered the military academies a long shot, and my thoughts at that time were focused on starting school at a small liberal arts college that I had never visited and of which I knew very little except for the recommendations and descriptions from Pop Scholl. I remember the pain of having to lose the sixty-dollar matriculation fee that I had deposited with URI when I withdrew my application (a lot of money in those days).

LEAVING HOME AND OFF TO COLLEGE

After returning home for a few days at the end of the summer, I packed a single suitcase and set off for Canton, New York by bus. My brother-in-law, Paul, drove me to the station in Providence, and as the bus drove off, I felt an immense loneliness for the first time in my life.

I know now that I was sustained by my prayers, my faith, and knowing that God was protecting me. I don't remember too much of the trip except that it was long, and I arrived in Canton very tired. I walked the short distance from the bus station to the college campus in the very small town. Excited and eager to start, I had arrived a few days early, and the dorms had not yet opened. I spent a few lonely days by myself in a room in the college sports complex before classes began.

When I stepped on that bus to go to St. Lawrence University, I left my boyhood home in Rhode Island at eighteen years old, never to really return again. I took with me incredibly happy and sad memories. Of the men and women outside my family who shaped my life during these years, I would list: Father DeAngelis (pastor), Larry Scalovino (scoutmaster), and all my teachers, but particularly, Sadie Cardin (sixth grade teacher), Marion Willard (high school music teacher), Elizabeth Duffy (high school English teacher), and Dom DiLuglio (high school football coach). And then, of course, Pop Scholl—a relative stranger who sized up my situation in such a short time and made the effort to get me a college scholarship. Each of these people set standards for me that have lasted a lifetime. Whenever there was some sort of gap in my life, one of them was there to fill it.

At St. Lawrence, I began to practice with the freshman football team, but after a few weeks, my elbow became badly infected from a cut I had received in a scrimmage. I had to drop football. I remember being very disappointed by this turn of events, but the thrust of academics and the need for additional money to sustain me became more pressing. My confidence was boosted by the good grades I had earned and by working two jobs (dormitory cafeteria and library).

It was at St. Lawrence that I first met Bob Ray, a fellow freshman, who would become a life-long friend and play a destined role in my life. We lived in different rooms along the third-floor corridor of the Men's Residence. I saw Bob on an almost daily basis.

During the rush season, Bob and I both joined fraternities that year (big part of the student culture then). We were also both enrolled in the Army Reserve Officer Training Corp Program (ROTC), where we attended classes and drilled together. At the time, neither of us knew that we would eventually pursue future military careers. Bob was to be commissioned from ROTC in 1956, and I would be commissioned from West Point in 1957. I lost contact with Bob after I left St. Lawrence at the end of freshman year to attend West Point, but by what I have come to see as a grand design (I do not believe in chance), we would meet again thirteen years later in Vietnam.

When the holiday break for Thanksgiving was approaching, I began to be concerned. I wanted to return home like the remainder of the student body and was not anxious to spend the holiday by myself in Canton. I somehow found the money to take the train home and back for Thanksgiving, but the cost of travel made a big dent in my "budget." When Christmas approached, I was fortunate to get a free ride home to Rhode Island, but for the return trip to Canton, I thought I could save some money and opted to hitchhike back with a fellow SLU student friend from my area. This resulted in a two-day journey full of uncertainty and hardship before we arrived back in Canton. I learned from this experience that hitchhiking in winter can be quite challenging.

I began 1953 with increased confidence and hope. By this time, I was adjusting to the college experience, although it was not the "college experience" I had always envisioned. The deception of poverty I lived in my youth had worn thin. By now, reality had set in, and I fully recognized the financial limitations set by poverty. I knew I was poor, and any climb out of poverty would be up to me. That realization encouraged me to persist in my college work schedule, study hard, and continue to get good grades.

CHAPTER 5
RISKY ADVENTURE

I WAS COMPLETELY SURPRISED and astonished when, in February of that year, I received two similar letters from Congressman Fogarty and Senator Pastore. They informed me that I had done sufficiently well on my civil service screening exam the past July to qualify as a third alternate for West Point. What this meant was that I was fourth in line to the principal candidate for that appointment.

For me to be accepted, the principal, first, and second alternate would all have to drop out or be disqualified in some way. This seemed like a steep hill to climb, but if I were still interested, I should present myself at the Boston Army Base on 4 March 1953 to take the West Point qualifying exams. The exams would take three days, consisting of academic, physical fitness, and psychological exams.

I faced another dilemma: Was it worth taking the time off from classes and work to travel from Canton to Boston? And how would I get there and back? In my financial straits, I knew I could only do this by hitchhiking, but I was a little more wary of taking to the road during the winter, especially after the bad experience of returning from Christmas break just two months before.

Once again, I trusted in myself, and my faith in God encouraged me that it would turn out all right. When I consulted Dean Brown, he was very understanding and encouraged me to take the exams. He gave me an excused absence from classes during this period, but he didn't advise me on how to get there and back.

With some trepidation, I began the adventurous hitchhike to Boston in early March. It turned out to be a risky thing to do and made me realize that God was really watching over me. With audacity and a degree of naiveté, I set off with my suitcase and a set of handmade signs naming the larger cities I had to pass through to reach Boston (Albany, Springfield). I dressed "Joe College" (jacket and tie), and, with very little money in my pocket and a road map, I stood by the side of the road and stuck out my thumb.

Somehow, I got the rides needed to eventually make it to Boston and return to Canton. I could use the word "fortunate" to describe this experience, but with the number of things that turned my way, I know it was not luck but divine providence that I made it there and back.

Of the many "fortunate" incidents that surrounded my hitchhiking trip to Boston, one involved "Turk" Petrarca, my boyhood companion and fellow altar boy at Sacred Heart Church. As a football star end, Turk was named high school all-state team and received a scholarship at Boston College. He was now attending his first year at BC. We had corresponded a few times over the past year, and when I wrote to him that I might be coming to Boston to take the West Point exams, he immediately sent me a post card to invite me to stay with him in his dorm room while I was there.

Since I had to plan my hitchhiking venture with some flexibility (I didn't know exactly how long it would take me to get there), I built in an extra day to arrive in Boston the day before the exams began. The army would quarter all the candidates in barracks at the Boston Army Base during the three days of the exam, so I had one possible night to worry about where I would sleep. On this basis, I wrote back to Turk to take him up on his offer to stay at least one night with him, but I warned him that I wasn't exactly sure when I would get there.

Another "fortunate" presence was the Novena Medallion to Mary that my sister had given me before I left for St. Lawrence. She told me to keep it on my person all the time and use it when I needed help. I always kept it in my wallet, and as I set out from Canton to Boston that wintry morning in early March, I took it out and placed it in my pocket. As I waited by the roadside with my Joe College get-up and signs, I would take out the medallion and say the designated prayers. I prayed for rides and for success in the exams and relied on the brashness of my youth to protect me. As I write this, I realize I should have been praying for my safety as well.

I was doing well on the rides, and the weather was not unbearable. I got to Albany, but the ride took me to the city outskirts, and I really had to get to the other side of the city to get the long-haul rides I was looking for. I somehow got through the city and on the road leading to Springfield/Boston, but I had lost quite a bit of time on my "schedule."

It was getting late in the afternoon, and I was losing daylight. Getting rides at night is a little more difficult, and I was beginning to worry when, finally, an eighteen-wheeler stopped and said he was going all the way to Boston. What luck—the signs had worked again. The driver told me to throw my suitcase in the back of his trailer since there was no room in the cab.

When I opened the trailer doors, it was completely empty. I felt a little foolish placing my suitcase on the floor of this big, empty trailer. The entire ride to Boston I heard my suitcase slide back and forth along the trailer floor and bang against the walls each time we braked or took an incline. I consoled myself that a scratched suitcase was a small price to pay for the blessing of this ride.

The driver was friendly, and when I told him what I was doing and where I was going, I felt even more "blessed" when he told me he would be going right by the Chestnut Hill area of Boston. Throughout the ride, I continued to silently pray the Novena to Mary and finger my medallion. The ride from Albany to Boston was at least six hours, and by the time we reached the outskirts of Boston, it was well after midnight. True to his word, the driver stopped at the foot of Chestnut Hill. Pointing upward, he said I would find the Boston College campus at the top.

MY MOTHER,
MY CONFIDENCE!

O Mary immaculate, the precious name of Mother of Confidence, with which we honor thee, fills our hearts to overflowing with the sweet consolation and moves us to hope every blessing from thee such a title has been given us then, it is a sure sign that no one has recourse to thee in vain. Accept, therefore, with a mother's love our devout homage, as we earnestly beseech thee to be gracious unto us in our every need. Above all do we pray thee to make us live in constant union with thee and thy divine Son Jesus. With thee as our guide, we are certain that we shall ever walk in the right way; in such wise that it will be our happy lot to hear thee say on the last day of our life those words of comfort: "Come then, my good and faithful servant, enter thou into the joy of thy Lord." Amen.

An indulgence of 500 days (S.C.Ind., Jan. 26, 1901 S.P. Ap., Aug. 8, 1936). The Raccolta 381.

Let us venerate our Blessed Mother under this title and often cry to her:

"MY MOTHER, MY CONFIDENCE!"
MATER MEA, FIDUCIA MEA.

An indulgence of 300 days (Benedict Xv, Jan. 27, 1917). The Raccolta 278.

Concordat cum originali,
Ioannes A. McMahon, S.T.D.

Gorman Church Goods House

Scan of the Novena to Mary I kept all these years

I retrieved my suitcase from the back of the trailer, thanked the driver profusely, and started walking up the hill. I had the postcard that Turk had sent me which gave me his room number in Liggett Hall. As I trudged up the hill with my suitcase, a police car drove by slowly, stopped, and backed up. He put his light on me and asked what I was doing out after midnight walking up Chestnut Hill.

I told him the whole story as succinctly as I could, wondering if he would believe me. At the end of my tale, he told me to get in the police car, and he drove me the rest of the way to Liggett Hall! I was fortunate to have run into a friendly cop, since it was still a good distance before reaching the dormitory.

After the policeman dropped me off at the front entrance, I still had to find Turk's room in this darkened building. I did have his room number, so I started down the halls looking at door numbers, and after some searching, I matched the number on the post card. I had gone this far on this adventure, and I wasn't going to stop now, so I screwed up my courage and knocked on the door. No response.

What should I do? Knock louder? Suppose this isn't the right room. What sort of response would I get from someone sleeping in the room that wasn't Turk Petrarca? How would I explain being there at this hour of the night?

I knocked slightly louder. No response. I knocked louder, and this time, I heard someone rustle inside the room and come to the door. It was a magic moment when the door opened, and there Turk stood, all six feet plus of him, in his underwear!

He yelled "Joe!" and I yelled "Turk!" at the same time. I spent the remainder of the night with Turk. The next day, I reported to the Boston Army Base and spent the next three days taking the exams.

After the exams, I began the return by thumb to Canton, reversing the order of the signs and making it through Albany before dark. Then things began to sour. A bad winter storm had developed, and my last ride took me to a little crossroads just below Watertown. (The New York State Thruway had not been built yet, and I had to use secondary back roads to get through Watertown to Canton.)

It was getting quite late by now, and I waited for several hours in that spot without getting a ride. The storm was getting worse, and only a very few cars were on the road. I began to get a little desperate, devising a plan to get out of the storm and find a place to sleep if I could not get a ride.

There was a tavern on the other side of the road where I planned to ask the owner if he would allow me to sleep in his place that night.

At midnight, just about the time I was deciding to make the move, the lights went out in the tavern, and I realized that I was quite alone at the crossroads. The wind and snow still howled about me, and there weren't many prospects for another car to come along. Time to finger the medallion and pray to Mary.

Sometime later, the lights of a car appeared through the blowing snow. I held up my sign for Watertown very high. The car passed slowly by me down the road with only the driver. There was always a better chance for a ride with someone traveling alone, but as I watched the taillights move away, my desperation intensified.

Suddenly, the brake lights went on, and the car began to back up. I ran toward the backing car, and when it stopped in front of me, the driver leaned over to the passenger side window and rolled it down a small crack. He had obviously locked all the car doors, not taking a chance on me. He yelled through the window, "What are you doing out on a night like this?"

Again, I had to tell my story as convincingly as I could. Again, I found someone who opened the door and let me in.

There is always an awkward period after getting a ride when both the driver and rider have to break through that bubble of trust. I guess I should have been as wary of him as he was of me, but I just didn't have the luxury of such concerns. It turned out that he was going as far as Watertown.

Remembering Pop Scholl lived in Watertown, I realized I might call him for help in what was becoming a desperate situation. So, I ventured, "Do you know Pop Scholl, the principal of the high school in Watertown?"

He immediately replied, "Of course I know Pop Scholl."

I then took another chance, "Do you know where Pop Scholl lives?

"Of course," he chuckled, "everyone in Watertown knows where Pop Scholl lives."

I found the ice broken, the trust now there. He drove me to Watertown and directly to Pop Scholl's home and dropped me off.

Once again on this adventure, I found myself knocking on a door well after midnight to ask someone to take me in. Once again, welcoming and loving friends, the Scholls, took me in, gave me a bed, fed me breakfast, and got me on a bus to Canton in the morning. All the talk the next day was about this being one of the worst winter storms the area had endured for a number of years. I now wonder at how many trying situations my prayers had gotten me through to make that trip possible.

OUT OF THE BLUE

Despite the risk I took in this harrowing experience, I still considered my chances of getting into West Point very low. Finishing my freshman year at St. Lawrence, I hitchhiked home to Rhode Island in May for summer work. I fully intended to return to Canton for my second year, even leaving a trunk of belongings in the dormitory attic of the Men's Residence since I planned to live there my second year and work as a dormitory rector. My freshman year at St. Lawrence had been rewarding and successful, and I was inspired with thoughts of future major fields of study. I particularly enjoyed and did well in biology, geology, and math courses, and a future in medicine or science seemed possible.

That summer I served as a cabana boy (general flunky, go-getter, and waiter for fifteen cabanas) at the Narragansett Dunes Club—an exclusive resort on the bay. I was a month into the job when the phone rang at my post. I thought it was another order from one of the cabanas for vichyssoise, but instead, the call was from my mother.

Brimming with excitement, she told me, "You received a letter from West Point—you've been accepted as a qualified alternate!" I could hardly believe it! (In order to fill entering classes, the best of the qualifying alternates are selected to round out spaces available.)

Mom continued, "It says report to West Point on 7 July 1953 to begin Beast Barracks."

That was only three weeks away! I informed my boss at the Dunes Club of the circumstances and immediately hitchhiked home. (How else?)

My dear and reliable brother loaned me the three-hundred dollars required for entry as the initial down payment on uniforms, and I immediately bought the pair of black shoes recommended in the letter, since it also advised that the shoes should be "broken in" prior to reporting. Neighbors, friends, and civic leaders from Natick hosted a wonderful testimonial banquet for me that I'll never forget. Heady stuff for a nineteen-year-old! I was ready to start my next unexpected adventure as I headed off to West Point.

CHAPTER 6
WEST POINT REMEMBERED

I COULD WRITE PAGES about my four years at West Point, but I will restrict my thoughts to the people and events that sustained and inspired me during those years.

Fathers Moore and McCormack were the priests during my time at West Point, and both were outstanding individuals who left their mark on generations of Catholic cadets. As a member of the Catholic Squad, I sang in the Catholic Choir. We made yearly trips to New York City to sing in St. Patrick's Cathedral. Cardinal Spellman always greeted us and gave us commemorative medals.

There were also members of the staff and faculty who influenced my development and outlook on life and the military. Captain William Cooper and Captain "Peachy" Keane were two of my company tactical officers. They were the regular army officers who looked after the discipline and order of my company of cadets. I consider myself privileged to have had these men as my leaders and role models.

The tactical officer in the adjoining cadet company, a major named Alexander Haig, was just beginning to make his mark in the army. I include a humorous account of Alexander Haig in the speech I gave as the "Old Grad" at the West Point Founder's Day Dinner in 2009 found in Appendix C.

Then there was a tall, lanky lieutenant colonel named Tom Rienzi on the regimental staff. He made a big impression on me then as a cadet and even more so later during my army career. My interactions with him in the Pentagon would inspire me to follow in his footsteps later when I entered the four-year formation process to become an ordained deacon in the Catholic Church.

Roommates were essential, sometimes even critical, to successfully completing the four years at West Point. After the academy's deliberate mixing of company mates as roommates during plebe year, a cadet was free to choose his own roommates for the remainder of his time at the academy. In my case, I chose to room with Dick Morton and Clancy Hall for those three years. This turned out to be a most serendipitous choice. We forged a bond that has lasted a lifetime.

ARMY BLUE

"The true love of my life, Sue Oebbecke, 'joined the Army too' on 20 July 1957"

West Point has a tradition of music and songs that truly weaves its way into the fabric of its history and lore and into the hearts of its graduates, certainly this one. One of the many cherished songs is *Army Blue*, a sentimental ballad with a rich academy history. In the third stanza, the ballad pays worthy tribute to the many cadet "drags" (dates) who faithfully and patiently visited their cadet beaus, and after marriage, they became part of the (then) distaff side of the Army:

> *To the ladies who come up in June,*
> *We'll bid a fond adieu,*
> *Here's hoping they be married soon,*
> *And join the Army too.*

From the first time I heard this ballad, I became caught up in that stanza, but never more so than at the time I was living and feeling it as a cadet.

I attribute the most memorable thing that happened to me at West Point to my roommate Clancy when, after some prodding and shenanigans, he and his fiancé, Doris Birchler, found a way to introduce me to Susanne Oebbecke, my future wife. I hesitate to use the trite sentiment "love at first sight," but for those who have been so smitten, the feeling is completely descriptive.

Sue dominated my thoughts and feelings after I first met her, and my plans for an evolving future in the army began to include her. Our somewhat brief courtship involved meeting again on the fifty-yard line at half time of the Army-Navy game that fall, and after that, almost steady dating on weekends for the remainder of my last year at West Point. Over this time, Sue had become a *fixed* part of all my future plans, and we decided to marry at West Point.

We began the marriage preparation process with Father Moore, who initially challenged us by suggesting we did not know each other long enough. This wise pastor was aware of just too many hurried cadet marriages that ended badly. Sue and I were able to convince him of the sincerity of our intent, and we set our marriage plans. Since cadets could not marry until after graduation, we resisted the temptation to get married on graduation day (4 June) as so many other classmates did. We just felt both special occasions needed their separate day. So, on 20 July 1957, Father Moore joined us in a very joyous, military-style marriage at the Most Holy Trinity Chapel.

Our happy day 20 July 1957

CHAPTER 7
NEW HORIZONS

". . . It launched a whole new world for me . . ."

SUE AND I HONEYMOONED in Maine and Canada, and then we started our great army adventure by driving to Lawton, Oklahoma. After finishing the Basic Artillery Course at Fort Sill, we next traveled to Fort Benning, Columbus, Georgia, for airborne (parachute) training. In late February 1958, we were finally ready to depart for our first permanent assignment to the 25th Infantry Division, Schofield Barracks, Territory of Hawaii.

Just before departing, we received the joyous news that Sue was pregnant. We drove cross-country to San Francisco and boarded the *Leilani* for a five-day Pacific cruise to Hawaii. While Sue was well prepared with pills in anticipation of sea and morning sickness, she never used a single one—but I certainly needed them!

JOYOUS EVENT

"Both our daughters were born Army Brats,
Susanne (Territory of Hawaii) . . ."

We spent over three years in Hawaii, longer than the usual tour. Our first daughter, Susanne—named after her mother—arrived on 6 October 1958. It was a time of great adjustment for us in many ways. Sue and I grew in our commitment to each other as we struggled with living on lieutenant's pay and learning to be new parents.

In retrospect, my initial military assignment proved to be typical for many who start at the bottom rung of any organization. I learned how to deal with people and successes and failures, all part of maturing. I found out that the West Point "army" and the real-life "army" were not the same. Somewhat disappointed and disillusioned, I seriously pondered my future career as an army officer. Eventually, I resolved that I wanted to stay committed to an army career, but I clearly wanted and needed something different.

In the post-Sputnik environment, the military services were very anxious to school officers in the sciences. I saw this as my opportunity to find something "different" to spark my career. It was then that I applied for army-sponsored advanced schooling. My academic background was not aimed toward the hard sciences. Despite this, I was accepted at Iowa State University in Ames for graduate schooling in physics. We departed Hawaii in July 1961, landed in San Francisco, and drove "home" cross-country to Philadelphia and Rhode Island to show our daughter to her grandparents for the first time. After a great leave at both our homes, we traveled halfway back across the country to Ames, Iowa, to begin study.

BE CAREFUL WHAT YOU ASK FOR

Our parish for the next two years was the student Neumann Center, and occasionally, St. Mary's Church in Ames. I needed two churches for all the prayers I was saying to get me through graduate school in physics! Our year group graduate class started with twenty-five people. Two years later when I graduated, we were down to three people. This was one of the most difficult periods of my life—and as I look back on it, for Sue as well.

After the first year, I was ready to give it all up. I was really struggling with the courses. My math always seemed to be six months behind my physics! I could only see another year of frustration ahead of me, and I was trying to spare my little family this self-imposed hardship. At my worse moment, when I came home from a two-hour exam with a splitting headache, I wrote a letter requesting release from the program. I showed it to Sue, and this turned out to be a shining moment for her. She tore up the letter and said we would not quit. She would rather we flunked out than quit! We then got down on our knees and prayed that God give us the strength and wisdom to continue.

There were no great bolts of lightning just then, but eventually, a quiet and gentle turning about did take place. I scraped through the first year with Cs. In the second year, I began my research with Dr. Clayton Swenson. He outlined a one-year project that could well qualify for a master's thesis and also greatly engaged me. It would require lab time and exploratory "runs" on his high-pressure physics apparatus. Dr. Swenson became my mentor, another in the long line of special people who came into my life just when I needed them.

My coursework started to pick up, and I saw my first graduate course A during the first semester of my second year. I spent a great deal of time in the laboratory that year learning to run the apparatus, and after I was ready, I began my series of runs to gather data for my paper. I ran into some problems right at the beginning, but with persistent help and patience from Dr. Swenson, we found the error and moved on.

The error caused some delay in the time I had been allotted on the laboratory apparatus. (It was one of a kind and being used by other graduate students under Dr. Swenson's mentorship.) In order to make up my time and stay on schedule, I had to conduct my "runs" over the Christmas vacation days. In fact, I was in the lab on Christmas Eve doing my final run. Right next to me was Dr. Swenson. We finished by midnight—a Christmas Eve I will never forget. This kind, remarkable man had the compassion to understand my struggles and to encourage and help me finish.

The final result was a paper worthy of the *Journal of Chemistry and Physics*, co-authored by Dr. Swenson and me.[1] I graduated in July of 1963 with a Master of Science degree. I don't think I've ever worked harder in my life. Walking with me to pick up my diploma that day were Sue and Dr. Swenson.

The army next assigned me to a "utilization tour" since they had sponsored my degree and wanted some value in return for my schooling. My orders read "USATECOM (US Army Test and Evaluation Command), Aberdeen Proving Ground, Maryland." After a well needed rest and leave to our homes in Philadelphia and Rhode Island, we made our way to the banks of the Chesapeake for our next assignment.

CHAPTER 8
ANOTHER LOOK AT THE ARMY

USATECOM WAS A NEW feature of the recently reorganized "corporate" army. It was a major command headed by a two-star general and staffed by many senior officers. Once again, I was at the bottom rung, but things were different here. I was given responsibilities and tasks to perform that had significant scope and impact on the army as a whole. Yet once more, I was "blessed" with a military boss, Colonel Lowell Thompson, who welcomed, guided, and gave me confidence in my new role.

My two years at USATECOM and Aberdeen Proving Ground brightened my outlook on the army and increased my conviction that I could have a career as an army officer. My horizons were broadened, and I was encouraged to pursue a future for myself and my family of three.

ANOTHER JOYOUS EVENT

". . . and Marly (Aberdeen Proving Ground) . . ." made four!

Sue and I always wanted to add to our family, but we discovered while in Iowa that Sue had a condition that prevented future pregnancy. She had an operation in Ames to correct the problem. Her doctor gave us the small possibility of her becoming pregnant within two years following the operation.

While at Aberdeen, the two years had passed, so we started the process of adopting a child. We had prayed fervently but eventually accepted this was God's will. We were well into the adoption process when the phone call came to me at work—Sue was pregnant! We were ecstatic with this turn of events. Our second daughter, Maria—who came to be called "Marly"—was born on 10 December 1964.

MOVING UP THE CAREER LADDER

I next received orders for the career course at the Chemical School, Fort McClellan, Alabama. We departed Aberdeen just prior to Christmas 1965, spent a wonderful Christmas with Sue's folks in Philadelphia, and set off for Alabama and a new phase of my army career.

The Chemical Officer Career Course is nine months of schooling in nuclear, biological, and chemical operations (NBC). Since I was the senior ranking officer (and the oldest), I was made class commander. I had the privilege of leading twenty-five very bright and talented officers.

One incident typifies the racial situation blighting our country at that time. The class had taken a field trip to Pine Bluff Arsenal in Arkansas and returned through the Mississippi Delta area. It was time for a break, and I asked the bus driver to stop at a roadside restaurant.

As we approached the window counter to give our orders, I was told by the young lady behind the counter that I could be served but the person behind me would have to be served at another place behind the restaurant. I frankly was confused and did not understand what she meant, and only when I turned to Captain Oliver "Ollie" Westry standing behind me did I realize the ugliness of what she was telling me.

Ollie, always the true gentleman, said it was okay with him. Then shame, bitterness, and anger engulfed me, and I told the group to get back on the bus. This group of US Army officers would have no part of this local "custom." I was learning more than NBC Operations in Alabama.

As the course approached completion, the class began to receive orders for our next assignments. Nine members of the class received orders for Vietnam. My orders were to remain at the school and become an instructor. It's difficult to explain my feelings and thoughts at that time, but I knew what I had to do.

There was an intense war going on in Vietnam involving more and more of the total army to fight the expansion of communism. I was a strong opponent of communism and believed in the domino theory. I sincerely felt it should be confronted and resisted wherever it raised its head.

If I was really sincere about an army career, I knew I had to be part of the army that was doing the resisting. Although I would likely be sent to Vietnam after my two-year tour of duty at the Chemical School, I wanted and needed to act now. After talking it over with Sue, I sent in a volunteer request right after the course finished to have my orders changed to Vietnam so I could join my nine other course mates.

FIRST CHEMICAL OFFICER CAREER CLASS
5 January - 29 July 1966
Fort McClellan, Alabama

THIRD ROW: Youngblade; Kimball; Craig; Kolch; Sellers; Holman; Vaughan; Sheetz; Hollis; Majewski.
SECOND ROW: Washington; Benchoff, Poleski; Heyman; Duncan; Miles; Moore; Folkert; Noles; Oberholzer; James.
FIRST ROW: Westry; Gardner; Spitzer; Brisker; Captain Tedeschi, Class Commander; Colonel Pike, Commandant; Lt Colonel Isaacs, Course Director; Mann; DeWhitt; Renaud; Shegog.

*Our Chemical School class photo—I am marked, as well as Westry
and Gardner mentioned in the book*

CHAPTER 9
CHANGE OF ORDERS

THE COURSE FINISHED WITH many happy memories and a strong bond of comradeship among these young officers and their families. We said our sad goodbyes, and my family set off for a vacation while I awaited a possible change in orders. When we returned a week later, I had new orders for Vietnam waiting for me. However, it would be a challenging schedule to meet.

As events would have it, my volunteer request for Vietnam reached the personnel center in Washington at the same time as the 1st Air Cavalry Division needed to replace the Division Chemical Officer ASAP due to an emergency curtailment of his tour. The increased tempo of chemical operations in Vietnam and the key role of the Division Chemical Officer prioritized such a request.

Filling the position quickly was vital, so though the position called for a lieutenant-colonel (O-5), and I was still a captain (O-3), this did not seem to matter to the requesting division. I had earlier been placed on the major (O-4) promotion list, and it was uncertain whether I would be promoted to major before or after I departed for Vietnam. I was clearly honored and overwhelmed by this opportunity but also concerned, at the same time, that the position was two grades above my present rank.

I eventually reasoned that, because things moved at a quicker pace during times of war, exceptions quite often rule, and I was caught up in one of those exceptions. This new assignment presented an exciting challenge. Facing me right away was the almost impossible task of getting my family moved in the time schedule required to make my port-of-call date, 1 September 1966.

THE WRENCH

My orders gave me about two weeks to relocate my family and report to Travis Air Force Base for travel to Vietnam. I decided to settle them in Rhode Island while I was in Vietnam for thirteen months so Sue and my two girls would have my family to support and help them the thirteen months I would be away. Those two weeks are a blur in my memory. We made a very hurried move from Alabama to a rental house in Rhode Island.

We had only a few days after the furniture arrived from Alabama to set up our household. The pace was hectic, and I will always regret the strain I placed on my family to get things in order before I departed. I wanted everything to be stable and as "normal" as possible before I left which was, in retrospect, an impossible goal.

On the afternoon I was scheduled to take the departing flight from Greene Airport, I was hanging curtains in the living room in one of my last attempts to make things right before I left. I was dressed in my combat fatigue uniform and socks because my orders read to report in combat fatigues to Travis Air Force Base in California for supposedly immediate travel to Vietnam. When time ran out on me that afternoon, I had to stop hanging curtains, lace up my combat boots, and take my family with me to the airport.

I can only imagine how often that dreadful departing scene at the airport took place for so many families during the Vietnam era.

Mine was no less heart wrenching and difficult. I realize now that my almost eight-year-old daughter Susanne was badly traumatized by this experience, and the results became evident soon after I left.

During the flight to California, a compassionate flight attendant recognized what was happening to me and tried to boost my morale. I tried to respond to her kindness, but I just couldn't do it. I was emotionally and physically exhausted, and I'm certain I showed it. The entire flight seemed to be one long, dark moment, and I began to question whether I had made the right decision to volunteer for Vietnam.

HURRY UP AND WAIT

I reported to Travis on 1 September on time in my combat fatigues as written in my orders and fully expected to immediately board another airplane bound for Vietnam. What a letdown when I found out I would not be leaving right away! To my utter dismay, I did not leave for Vietnam until 6 September. My morale really took a nosedive as I waited with nothing to do but eat meals and make telephone calls home for the next five days.

I just could not understand why I had put my family through such an ordeal for the past two weeks to meet the reporting date only to be marooned on an air force base with nothing to do. Not a very good start to my Vietnam tour of duty, as I painfully began to realize that, in time of war, the individual is always secondary to the needs of the service. One service imperative was telling me to get to Travis Air Force Base at all costs so I could be sent to Vietnam as soon as possible; another service imperative said we'll send you there when we're ready. I clearly was caught in the middle.

I finally departed for Vietnam at noon on 6 September aboard a chartered flight. The airplane promptly broke down after less than two hours in the air, and we had to land in Seattle, where the entire manifest of 140 military passengers were put up for the night at a nearby airport motel. We took off again the next morning, 7 September, for a long and somber flight with two stops along the way, finally landing at Saigon at 3 a.m., also on 7 September. We had crossed the international date line and experienced the normal confusion of "losing a day."

Although 7 September turned out to be a very long day for me, it was also eventful because I was promoted to major that day as well. Essentially, I got on the airplane at Travis as a captain and got off the airplane in Saigon as a major. All this was consistent with the earlier promotional considerations leading to my assignment above grade in rank, but it also created more confusion and delay at the reception depot in Saigon (known as Camp Alpha or the "repot depot").

What are known as "by name" orders assigned me as a major to become the Division Chemical Officer of the 1st Air Cavalry Division at An Khe. But that meant nothing to the administrators at the reception depot. I was wearing captain's bars on my uniform, and they saw me only as a captain, despite all my protestations and explanations.

I was caught up in the individual versus the needs of the service dilemma once again. I was "raw meat" to them, and they were determined to send me to the Delta Region to the 25th Infantry Division. They were short of captains, and since they thought I was a commodity for reassignment, they had authority and were prepared to do it.

It took five more days of communicating back and forth with the military personnel staff back in the US to sort things out. I spent those five days in more anguish and frustration as I tried to make my way to the war. Camp Alpha was the worst place to spend this time, as I had to billet in somewhat crude temporary barracks which housed people both coming to Vietnam and those going home after completing their thirteen-month tours. The war stories being bantered about in the barracks were not confidence building to those waiting for assignments.

MAKING MY OWN WAY TO THE FRONT

On 12 September, I finally received the reception depot's approval of my orders, but they also informed me they could not arrange transportation to get me to An Khe until 14 September. That was the last straw! I was not going to wait two more days to arrive at my final destination, and I decided to make my own travel arrangements.

When I told the camp administrators what I wanted to do, they suggested I check in at the Tan San Nut Airbase nearby, which I did. Eventually I "bummed" a ride on a C-123 airplane with a planeload of cargo going to An Khe. The crew chief strapped me in with the rest of the cargo as a "passenger." I finally reached An Khe on 12 September, worn out but ready to go to war.

DIVISION CHEMICAL OFFICER

Upon notice of my surprise and unconventional arrival two days ahead of schedule, members of my chemical staff section drove to the airfield to greet me. Arrival at any new assignment as the new "boss" can be a challenge but even more so under the conditions I faced. I was filling the position of the Division Chemical Officer that had been vacant for at least two months. Beyond that, the role calls for a lieutenant colonel O-5, but I was a brand-new major O-4 still wearing O-3 captain's bars.

My staff consisted of an Assistant Division Chemical Officer (calls for a major O-4 but being filled by a captain O-3) and two CBRE Team Leaders (calls for and were being filled by captains O-3). It was not unusual then because of the rapid tempo of the war to have TOE (Tables of Organization and Equipment) positions filled by undergrade personnel. Since I was still wearing captain's bars when I arrived, one of the first things I did upon arriving at An Khe was to have major leaves sewn on my uniforms to at least dispel some of the confusion in rank!

I spent the next three weeks getting oriented and trying to fit into my new role as Division Chemical Officer. As an individual replacement, I missed the advantages I might have had if I had been part of the major unit move which took place when the 1st Air Cavalry Division relocated from Fort Benning to Vietnam just a year before in September 1965. In that case, I would have been already integrated and familiar with the command structure, personnel, and staff operations.

I had a great deal of catching up to do, and I set out to overcome this disadvantage. I wanted to get a feeling for the area of operations and how the role of the Division Chemical Officer fit in. To do this, I engaged in the ongoing division operations right away.

My first division chemical activities involved an elaborate enemy hospital located deep in a tunnel. In the ensuing search of this complex underground facility consisting of many tunnel branches, I was asked to confirm the use of smoke grenades to flush out the inhabitants. Unfortunately, several female nurses refused to exit and had been killed by suffocation.

Another maze of tunnels was discovered nearby, and I participated in their destruction with explosives. Where this was impractical, we "seeded" them with a powder form of CS (a component of tear gas) to hinder future use and occupation.

In another issue, the base camp had been attacked several times prior to my arriving and needed to be defended, but the huge perimeter would take a great deal of manpower to completely defend. To conserve manpower, manned strong points with designated fields of fire were established. Keeping the lines of sight open required cutting back the vegetation around the perimeter frequently, again requiring scarce manpower.

The chemical platoon assigned to the division solved the problem with GI ingenuity by rigging a spray boom to the strut of a helicopter and using the defoliant Agent Orange to control the growth of the vegetation. This was well before we recognized the damaging effects of Agent Orange on humans, and I look back in dismay at the lack of precautions taken by those handling it. Regretfully, part of the spraying of the perimeter also took out the banana crop of a nearby farmer, and I became involved in the compensation claim we approved to repay him for his loss.

My tasks were made easier by discovering some of the people I already knew there. I had two West Point classmates, John Hocker and Bill Seely, on the division headquarters staff, and I knew I could always rely on them. To my great delight, on one of the first days there, I also met another old friend, Major Bob Ray, from my St. Lawrence school days. Since Bob was also a member of the division staff, we ran into each other in the headquarters' mess hall. Thirteen years had passed since I had last seen Bob at St. Lawrence, but we recognized each other right away, and our warm friendship resumed as if it had never stopped.

Bob more or less "took me under his wing" for part of those three weeks as I was trying to get oriented to my duties and the warfront in Vietnam. As the Assistant G-5 (Chief of Staff for Civil Affairs), he had ready access to helicopter flights. On at least two occasions, he took me along to observe the type of work he was doing in the ongoing major operations the division was conducting at that time.

The first operation was called Operation Thayer, which ended on 1 October and was immediately followed by Operation Irving beginning the next day. The objective of these operations was to eliminate the influence of the People's Army of Vietnam and the Vietcong in Binh Dinh Province on the central coast of South Vietnam. As part of these operations, the division set up a Forward Operating Base (FOB) at a place called LZ (Landing Zone) Hammond. Elements of the division headquarters, to include Bob and I, were sent forward on 2 October, and we traveled for most of that day with the motor convoy that took us from An Khe to LZ Hammond.

MY BRIEF VIEW OF THE WAR

I spent 3 October with Bob Ray, and we flew to a nearby village and observed its entire population being herded by elements of the Vietnamese army into a sports stadium for relocation. About one hundred men, women, children, and even animals were being taken from their village, screened by the Vietnamese army for elements of the Vietcong, and then relocated to another village. This was one of the methods being employed to fulfill the mission of Operation Irving which was to eliminate the influence of the enemy.

There I came face to face with the harsh realities of the nature of the war we were fighting in Vietnam. It was a difficult scene for me to take in. Although it was part of Bob's G-5 assigned duties to be part of the US presence on site to monitor this activity, I know it was difficult for him as well.

As we walked through the groups of people, we noticed an older woman with a rough, bloodied bandage around the upper part of her leg. We stopped to check on her condition, and, with no interpreter, we were able to talk her into removing the bandage so we could determine her condition. As she unwrapped the bandage, we saw that she had packed and placed a large leaf over a bullet hole badly in need of repair. Bob immediately called for medical assistance from the Vietnamese soldiers assisting in the relocation.

When we returned to FOB Hammond at the end of that day, I had a message waiting for me. Although I had been forward for only two days, I was being summoned back to the division base camp at An Khe to coordinate future division chemical operations.

As was the practice, courier flights were established between the division base camp at An Khe and the forward operational sites using short take-off and landing (STOL) aircraft. Our forces employed the two-engine, high-wing C-7, known as the Caribou, built by de Havilland in Canada for this purpose. These flights satisfied several practical needs such as routine medical evacuation, personnel rotation, and other administrative requirements such as my need for transport back to An Khe.

In an ongoing Pentagon dispute for battlefield air space mission and control, the army had recently traded the Caribou to the air force for army ownership of most rotary wing aircraft.[2] In fact, army markings were still on the Caribou that day, but the aircraft was being operated by a four-man transition crew consisting of three air force members and one army crew member.

Scheduling a flight back to the base camp for my meeting was not complicated. After informing my boss, the G-3 (Chief of Staff for Operations), of my need to return to the base camp, I located the landing strip that had been cleared near the Division Command Post and placed my request for a flight with the small ground detachment that was operating the airstrip. I was told that I would take the morning flight the next day (one of two flights "scheduled" each day) and to be at the air strip by 0700.

PART 2
THE UPHEAVAL

CHAPTER 10
4 OCTOBER 1966

". . . In Vietnam, 1966, I experienced one of those life-altering events: I survived as a passenger when the Caribou aircraft flew into the side of Hon Cong Mountain at An Khe . . ."

I WAS AWAKE EARLY the next morning (4 October 1966), mostly because we spent the night anticipating a mortar attack (which did not occur), and I got very little sleep. Just as I was getting up, the division's Catholic chaplain poked his head in my tent and asked if I wanted to attend the Mass he was about to celebrate. I thought this was a good idea, and as it turned out, there were only two of us attending the Mass in addition to the priest. The other person was Bob Ray who, unknown to me at the time, had also scheduled himself to return that day to the base camp at An Khe.

Following Mass where Bob and I both received Communion, I made my way to the airstrip and waited for the STOL aircraft along with about thirty other people. To my surprise, I found Bob Ray waiting there as well. This was the first time I realized he would be on the same flight going back to An Khe.

The airstrip was just that—a strip-of-earth runway the military engineers had carved with bulldozers out of the highland jungle. It had an air sock and an operations shack in a converted CONEX shipping container at one end housing the ground crew and communications equipment. We were in the beginning of the monsoon season, and the day was overcast with thick, low-hanging clouds, and raining slightly. After a while, we were told that the morning flight had been canceled because of the poor visibility and that we should check back at 1500 for the afternoon flight.

I have only a vague recollection of how I spent the rest of that day before the flight. I remember visiting the headquarters Tactical Command Post and having a talk with the Assistant G-3, my classmate John Hocker, to review the tactical situation. Around 1500, Bob Ray and I were back at the airstrip along with about thirty-one other men (officers and enlisted) waiting for the aircraft to arrive from An Khe. The only administrative control action I remember was filling out a 3x5 card with name, rank, serial number, and unit, which was collected by the ground crew at the airstrip.

The weather was still bad, still slightly raining, and the airplane was delayed. It seemed that the flight was going to be canceled again when, in the distance, we heard the sound of the approaching aircraft. It made one low pass over the airstrip, passed out of sight again in the overhanging cloud banks, and then reappeared on the far side of the airstrip for its final landing approach. I had never actually seen a STOL aircraft land or take off, although I had seen films of them in operation. I was highly impressed by the very small amount of landing strip it needed to come to a stop, engines roaring in reverse, and then turn sharply around to load passengers.

RUSH TO THE FRONT

The aircraft stopped in front of the assembled group of passengers and lowered its rear cargo ramp. This seemed to be the signal that most of the passengers were looking for, and they rushed to board the aircraft through the lowered ramp. Some of these passengers were returning to base camp at An Khe to begin the process of rotating home, since they had completed their thirteen-month tours in Vietnam. Their rush to get on the aircraft turned out to be tragic.

A Caribou with later air force markings

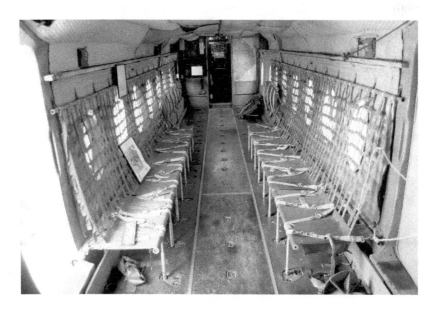

Interior of the Caribou

Unaware of the significance of their actions, seating location on the aircraft turned out to be a factor in determining survivability. The aircraft had bucket seats attached to both inner walls of the fuselage with approximately sixteen seats along each side. Those who rushed on first moved from the rear to the front of the aircraft in good military order and took the front seats. Bob Ray and I knew we had seats, so we strode leisurely over. The last to board, we took the two remaining bucket seats on the port (left) side of the aircraft, Bob in the last seat and me next to him.

We also had two injured soldiers requiring medical evacuation on board, including one stretcher case. The soldier in the stretcher appeared to have a broken leg, but he did not seem particularly in pain at the time. The loading of the soldier on the stretcher was causing some problems since his stretcher would have taken three bucket seats along the side of the aircraft if it was to be buckled in properly with safety straps. That would require the same number of anxious passengers to give up their seats to accommodate a secure installation.

To the best of my recollection, a quick decision was made (I feel certain by the air crew) not to give those three seats up but instead to lay the stretcher down the middle of the aircraft (just inside the cargo ramp). This arrangement left the injured soldier and his stretcher unsecured with the young army crewman kneeling behind the soldier, holding the top of the stretcher for stability. Most of the men were armed with either rifles (M-16s) or side arms. The men with rifles held them between their legs with the butts of the rifles on the floor of the aircraft and the muzzles leaning against their bodies or pointing toward the roof.

THE FLIGHT TO AN KHE

The cargo ramp was finally closed, and the airplane took off using about the same minimum runway it used to land. This was my first flight in a Caribou, and I can remember being impressed by its two powerful engines, its STOL capabilities, and its maneuverability. However, after a short while in the bucket seats, I realized this was clearly a military aircraft designed for function and not comfort. The approximate one-hour flight back to the base camp at An Khe seemed somewhat routine. Flying through thick clouds, the beginning of the stormy weather associated with the monsoon season in Vietnam, I felt some bumps and observed the cabin.

Being strapped in with the safety belt to my bucket seat, I noted the difference in buckles between the military safety belt and the commercial belt used on civil aviation aircrafts. In a civilian aircraft, you might take off your belt once the plane is up to altitude, but chatting with Bob Ray, I noted he kept his safety belt on during the flight as well. My mind kept occupied thinking about the upcoming meeting on coordinating chemical operations.

I couldn't help but observe with caution the young blond army crewman attending to the injured soldier in a stretcher. He kneeled unrestrained at the head of the stretcher. He rode the entire flight in this position, holding on to the rear of the stretcher, only occasionally getting up to look out the aircraft window. Later, this was revealed to be the army member of the flight crew, SP4 Bird, who was filling in for a friend with a birthday that day. The young, injured soldier in the stretcher did not say much during the flight.

The two lines of soldiers in bucket seats on either side of the aircraft held their rifles in front of them. Some of the soldiers talked quietly amongst themselves; others were more boisterous, especially those who were returning to the base camp for rotation home. The cabin was somewhat dark with no interior lights and only some daylight subdued by the cloud cover coming through the aircraft windows. The light shifted about, casting shadows with each turn of the aircraft.

The sergeant aircraft crew chief stood between the pilots occupying the two seats in the small cockpit cabin. He had apparently given up his seat as well to accommodate the passengers. Seated at the rear of the airplane, I could see the pilots inside the cockpit cabin—either there was no door to the cabin or the door was open, I don't recall. The crew chief was standing on the floor of the aircraft, leaning through the opening to the cockpit cabin on its raised platform so that his arms stretched across the backs of both pilot's seats.

It all seemed so casual and routine. The sergeant seemed to be having an animated discussion with the pilots during the flight. These are the last recollections I have of the state of the aircraft and its occupants just before the crash.

A ROCK IN THE CLOUDS

The subsequent events seemed almost instantaneous at the time, and I have only made some sense of what happened later after I learned the details of the crash. There was a sudden and loud roar of the engines, and the aircraft began to pitch violently upward. In the very next instance, I heard a shattering bang on the right side of the aircraft, and I began to be propelled up from my bucket seat. This was followed immediately by a second, much greater noise—truly indescribable but giving meaning to the word "crash." I felt myself being hurled forward and up at the same time, and then came an instant of blackness followed by complete silence.

I don't know how long the silence lasted, but in my next moment of cognition, I found myself lying on the side of a football "pile up" of people and bucket seats. My seat belt and bucket seat were wrapped around me, and I was confused and completely disoriented. Facing toward the back of the aircraft, I could see sky and daylight through an opening at the top of the airplane, but nothing was moving. There was this silence and no motion, and I slowly began to realize that the airplane must have come to a complete and sudden stop.

A moment before, I had been sitting at the rear left side of the aircraft, traveling at a high rate of speed. Now, an instant later, the airplane was motionless, and I was lying in what I judged to be the middle of the aircraft on a tangle of people, seat belts, and bucket seats that had totally filled the front of the cabin from floor to ceiling. The space from where I was lying in the middle of the airplane to the rear of the airplane was completely clear, empty of everything that had been there a moment before.

I then began to hear moaning and groaning noises from inside the football pile of people behind me. I realized that I was pressed against the injured soldier who had been in the stretcher on the floor of the aircraft in front of me. He had a bloody gash on his forehead and was moaning in pain. Then suddenly, I felt someone moving from the top of the pile of people, pushing himself over me and half crawling, half running for the open space at the rear of the aircraft.

Initially confused and disoriented, my mind became clear at this point, and I have concluded that I really never blacked out completely. I'm certain that I was one of only a few people not knocked unconscious by the crash. The moment of blackness I experienced must have been the short instant of time I was being hurled forward and up at the same time, and I had no control of my body or what was happening to me. My confusion and disorientation were enhanced by the fact that I was now lying on the ceiling of the upside-down aircraft.

Interior after crash, courtesy of Mike Zimmerman @ Jim4Jet.com

What I was seeing as an opening in the upper back of the airplane was the space where the cargo ramp should have been. The cargo ramp had broken loose during the crash, creating a skylight effect that was so incongruous to me at the time that it only added to my disorientation. None of us who were conscious realized exactly how we were now lying on the ceiling of the aircraft. We all had to learn the details later.

What we all later learned was that the aircraft had been flying through solid cloud cover on a ground-controlled approach (GCA) to the base camp airfield at An Khe (a fairly sophisticated airfield operation considering the wartime conditions). The pilot had received permission to land, lowered the landing gear, and made his final approach. There are a number of accounts attempting to explain the difficult circumstances; however, in the end, the pilot was on a landing path approach exactly parallel to the airfield runway two miles *east* of the correct runway landing path approach. This bearing led directly into Hon Cong Mountain, the dominant terrain feature overlooking the huge 1st Cavalry Division Base Camp and airfield at An Khe.

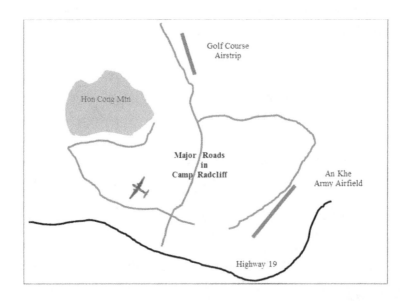

Map by Dr. John Thiel created for his "A Rock in the Clouds" report based on this initial manuscript, published for the Chemical Corps Hall of Fame (used with permission)

The mountain and the aircraft were completely enclosed in low-hanging clouds. The pilot continued through these blinding clouds, thinking he was lined up with the airfield runway, expecting to break out of the clouds at some minimum altitude, see the runway, and land. (Some of the circling we did earlier was a first attempt by the pilot to land that was aborted for a second try.) Instead, what the pilot saw right in front of him at that horrifying last instance were the trees and forest on the side of Hon Cong Mountain coming at him quickly. His last desperate reaction was to yank back on the wheel and gun the engines in an attempt to climb out of this certain head-on crash. (This explains the roaring of the engines I heard.)

Although the airplane responded quickly and began to pitch up, at almost the same instance, the right wing of the aircraft hit a tree and was torn off (the first bang I felt through the floor of the aircraft). The engine thrust from the left side, causing the aircraft to roll violently clockwise and hurling me upward and forward almost at the same time. Now upside down, our plane plowed into the side of the mountain (the "crash").

At the crash site, a large mahogany tree split the front third of the airplane, and clearly what had been an airplane flying at landing speed was brought to a complete and very sudden stop. The airplane had burrowed itself into the side of the mountain, upside down, one wing intact and the other snagged on nearby treetops.

Everything inside the airplane traveling at the same speed as the aircraft tried to continue at that speed, hurtling forward with great force and violence. This explains the "clean" airplane that resulted from the force of the impact. Obviously, the crash had exceeded the loading specifications of the bucket seats attached to the side of the aircraft, and these all gave way with the occupants still strapped in them, piling up and filling the middle of the aircraft from floor to ceiling.

The following photos I received from Bob Ray after he returned to service that year. The first three photos show different vantage points of the tail and the door I mention in my crash account. The fourth is the view from the wreck site; the fifth is the US Army marking on the severed wing; and the final photo is what we can only assume is the front, buried in the tree overgrowth. There is a marking of "propeller" on the final image identifiable only by zooming in.

Approaching the crash site

Tail of the Caribou

Front of image: A large mahogany tree crushed the front of the aircraft
Back of image: The door we opened to signal for help above the wing

View of Camp Radcliffe from the crash scene

Wing showing army markings, possibly the one that was broken off

Digital zoom reveals "propeller" in lettering

CHAPTER 11
EVALUATING THE AFTERMATH

THERE WAS NO EXPLOSION or fire. Considering the violence and force of the crash, this was extraordinary. Whatever the reason, it was a miracle, because, as it turned out, I doubt that any of us would have been able to escape a burning airplane. Which brings me back to the one person who did exit the aircraft immediately following the crash. Apparently, this one soldier found himself in the middle of the football pile of people, struggled to free himself, and then scrambled his way out of the aircraft. He was the individual who crawled over me to get to the open space at the rear of the aircraft where the cargo ramp had been.

I had the presence of mind to yell at him to stop, come back, and help the rest of us. Instead, he continued to scramble right through the open space and disappeared. From later accounts, it appears this was the one army member of the flight crew, SP4 John T. Bird. When the rescuers arrived, he was found dead under the wing. I can only surmise that SP4 Bird survived the crash with serious injuries but initially not severe enough to prevent him from escaping the aircraft.

ASSESSING INJURIES

The following events took place in roughly this order in the approximately thirty-minute interval between the time of the crash and the arrival of help. The time was now around 1600, and daylight was beginning to fade.

I first unwrapped myself from the entanglement of seat belts and bucket seats to move away from the pile of people. It was only then, when I began to move, that I realized I was injured. As much as I tried, I could not move my right leg—it simply would not go where I wanted it to go. I had no control of it. I really did not feel any great pain, but I was essentially immobilized and felt very awkward.

(Afterwards, I surmised that if I really had to make it through that opening in the back of the airplane to escape a fire or explosion, I might have been able to do it. However, I also later learned that the opening through the cargo ramp was ten to twelve feet off the ground, and I'm not sure how I would have managed the jump with my leg in that condition. I'm glad I did not have to experience that challenge.)

At the time, my self-diagnosis was that my leg was broken at the femur. When the first medical help arrived on the scene, they also treated it as a broken leg. It was only after X-rays at the base camp field hospital that it was diagnosed correctly—a dislocated leg bone and broken hip. I later learned that this is a classic injury in a front-end automobile collision where the driver's leg or legs are driven back by the impact of the crash through the acetabulum (hip socket), breaking off a piece of the cup-shaped bone that holds the femur in the hip socket.

In my case, the impact of the right wing of the airplane hitting the tree was transmitted through the floor of the aircraft to my right leg, causing the same kind of injury. Why my left leg and hip socket did not suffer the same injury is a mystery to me. With the femur out of the hip socket, the leg simply cannot move, which explains my immobility. My only other injury was a superficial cut on my face that bled slightly.

HELPING OTHERS

My first concern since I was conscious was to help others. I was able to move my body and upper torso a little, by reaching down and moving my right leg with my hands. To my right, I saw Bob Ray on the floor wrapped in his seat belt and bucket seat. He was alive and moaning, holding his stomach with both hands. I was able to free him from his seat belt and tried to get him to talk. He could only mumble at this point. His face was completely white, and I feared he was going into shock. He drew his knees up in a fetal position. I could see no external wounds or injuries.

Bob was one of the first people to be transported to the base camp hospital for treatment after the rescue. The seat belt digging into his stomach during impact had ruptured his intestines so that he was hemorrhaging internally. This explained his white face and why I could see no injuries. While the seat belt caused the injury, it probably saved Bob's life. I don't know how much the seat belt had to do with my injury—possibly some since the belt went from my left shoulder to my right hip where my injury took place. I believe, however, the seat belt also saved my life, despite the fact that the bucket seat gave way during the impact.

At the base camp hospital, Bob went immediately into surgery, and a large section of his intestine was removed. He survived this ordeal, but not without some real trepidation and concern for his life. His condition was so serious that army officials sent for his wife and three children to join him in the hospital in Japan where he was transferred for recovery. Bob did recover and later returned to Vietnam to complete his tour of duty. He completed a distinguished military career and retired in Annandale, Virginia.

Next, I tried to help the soldier in the stretcher who was behind me in the pile of people. Somehow, I got myself away from the pile-up by crawling and using my hands to pull my right leg along. I pulled the soldier away from the pile and laid him down. He was alive but very incoherent. I knew I had to stop the bleeding from the gash on his forehead. I surmised there were first aid kits onboard the aircraft and yelled out for one, though I didn't know if anyone would respond.

A voice to my left said there was one near him; he plopped a first aid kit over next to me. It comforted me to know there was one other conscious person nearby. I opened the kit and found a large bandage which I unwrapped, applied, and fixed to the soldier's wound on his forehead.

The pilot, co-pilot, and crew chief, who had to endure the shock and horror of that last-second view of the mountain directly in front of them, were all killed. How the injured soldier on the stretcher, not secured to the plane in any way, escaped the same fate is a mystery. The gash on his forehead showed he must have hit something as he was thrown forward.

I began to hear other voices and activity among the groaning pile behind me. The one voice that will haunt me forever is that of the soldier who somehow could see me through the pile of people, but I could not see him or get to him. His cries were, "Help me! Help me! Major, please help me! My rifle is through my stomach. Help me or I'll bleed to death. Please help me!" I could only surmise that he was one of the soldiers I saw down the line of seats with his rifle out in front of him. I was completely helpless. I knew there was no way I could get to him through that pile of people and twisted bucket seat frames. I could not stand and could hardly crawl.

After a while, his cries became more feeble and then stopped altogether. When the first rescuers arrived, I was able to tell them immediately about the soldier in the pile with the rifle through his stomach. I saw them locate him in the pile, isolate him outside the aircraft, and stabilize his condition.

The rescuers had the incredibly good sense not to pull the rifle out. Instead, they took off the stock group and wrapped the remainder of the rifle in place to the soldier's body. I eventually learned that this soldier, Daniel R. Madden, made it to the base camp hospital alive, went immediately into surgery, and had the barrel of the rifle removed under operating room conditions. It is certain he would have died if the rescuers had tried to remove the rifle from his stomach at the crash site. Part of the miracle was that, while the rifle had truly penetrated through the soldier's body, it missed his spinal cord. Although he lost part of his intestine and spleen, he would make a complete recovery.

DISTRESS SIGNAL

At some point, I made contact with the voice to my left that threw out the first aid kit. A soldier crawled away from the pile and sat down, looking dazed, next to the door of the aircraft. From what I could observe, he did not have any visible injuries. From correspondence I received twenty-one years after the crash, I feel certain this soldier was Sergeant Jordan Brindley.

In our brief initial conversation, we both recognized and acknowledged in the most grateful terms that we had just survived an airplane crash. We also discussed whether anyone would know we were down, and we wondered whether we were inside the base camp perimeter or outside the perimeter in Vietcong territory. The last point made me check my .45 caliber pistol still strapped to my web belt. Then I realized that we might be able to draw any would-be rescuer's attention to us by firing my pistol outside the door using the universal distress signal (a series of three-shot bursts), or it might draw the wrong kind of attention from the Vietcong.

I opted for taking a chance with would-be friendly rescuers, and I asked the soldier to open the airplane door next to him. The soldier grabbed the door handle and pushed down as hard as he could from his sitting position, but the door would not open. He tried several times; still, it would not budge. Trying to figure out why, this is when we began to realize that the airplane was upside down and we were lying on the ceiling and not the floor of the airplane. With the airplane upside down, our minds finally registered that the door handle had to be moved in the opposite direction to open. When the soldier pushed up, the door finally opened.

Since the soldier was closest to the door, I took my pistol out of the holster and told him to lean out the open door and fire the distress call. I presumed the soldier knew how to handle and fire the .45 caliber pistol, so I handed it to him with a full clip, handle grip out. (We were practically right next to each other with Bob Ray lying to my right front.)

He grasped the pistol by the handle with one hand, and instinctively drew the slide back with his other hand while the barrel of the pistol pointed right in my face. Drawing the slide back on a .45 caliber pistol places a bullet in the chamber, and it only takes a trigger pull to fire. The moment seemed to be frozen in time for me. Here I had just survived an airplane crash, and now I had a loaded, ready-to-fire pistol pointed between my eyes at a distance of a couple of inches. That couple of seconds seemed like an eternity to me. I have this picture of the soldier next to me with an armed pistol in my face, and I'm not too sure of his mental or physical state since he also just survived an airplane crash. I know that I very carefully and very deliberately reached up and moved the pistol away from my face. I did not want to be killed by a small arms accident just after I survived an airplane crash! The moment passed as quickly as it came.

The soldier leaned out the door and fired several three-round bursts until there were no more bullets. There was a brief moment of silence after the last shot, and then a loud cry from Bob Ray on the floor. I thought Bob was unconscious at this point, so it startled me when I heard him yell, "Don't fire that pistol! There may be gas fumes, and it could cause an explosion!"

I guess Bob was conscious most of the time, at least long enough to hear our conversation about firing the pistol and attracting would-be rescuers. I am still amazed that Bob had the presence of mind to warn of safety precautions considering his pain and physical condition at that time.

LIMITED PERSPECTIVE

In addition to the events described above, I know I spent some time trying to analyze our situation and consider what to do next. I knew we must be close to the base camp because of our attempts to land just prior to the crash. I knew one person had escaped from the airplane, but where did he go, and was he in a better or worse position by running away from the downed aircraft?

No one else appeared to be in any condition, physically or mentally, to exit the aircraft and seek help. I was never able to ascertain the extent of the injuries of the soldier who shot my pistol outside the airplane door, but it was clear that he preferred to stay with the airplane and the chance of rescue. I could tell, too, that in addition to the low-hanging clouds and rainy conditions, we were beginning to lose sunlight. I had to face the prospect of spending the night in a crashed airplane with everybody either dead or injured and just two or three conscious people.

I had no idea we had crashed into the side of a mountain or what the condition of the airplane or crash site were like. All I knew was what I could see from inside the airplane through the now open door and the skylight-like space where the cargo ramp had been.

I began to think about stories of the atrocities in World War II where retreating allied forces had to leave medical personnel behind treating the wounded, but both were usually killed by the Japanese. I imagined if the Vietcong found us first, they would not bother to take prisoners or care for the wounded either. I had convinced myself we would all be killed on the spot. This caused me to retrieve my pistol and to put in another full clip of ammo. I was determined that I was not going to be killed in a passive manner. I will be forever grateful that I did not have to ponder this situation too long. In approximately thirty minutes, I heard noises and American voices outside the airplane.

Salvaging party at the crash site after the rescue

CHAPTER 12
VERTICAL RESCUE

THOSE WERE THE LONGEST thirty minutes I spent in my life. The airfield at the base camp knew we were down because we had disappeared from the radar screen. Also, as we were flying in circles prior to landing, and especially on what the pilot thought was his final leg before landing, we flew over a base camp petroleum dump at An Khe. We learned later that the soldiers manning the petroleum dump heard us fly directly overhead (although they could not see us in the low, overhanging clouds), and they knew from the sound of the engines and the direction we were headed that we were flying directly into the mountain. A number of these soldiers began climbing up the side of the mountain in the direction of the airplane engine noise even before the crash took place. These soldiers were among the first rescuers to arrive on the crash scene. (See chapter 24, "Other Witnesses on the Scene" for my later communications with an MP on the scene.)

I yelled from inside the airplane to the rescuers that we needed help right away. I heard the sound of people climbing aboard the aircraft either through the door or the cargo ramp. The first face I remember was that of an African American soldier asking me where I was hurt. I told him I was not critically injured (I barely even registered the pain yet), and others needed help right away like Bob Ray, the soldier in the stretcher, and most of all, the soldier with the rifle through his stomach. By this time, others had climbed into the airplane as well. At some point, I can remember being injected with morphine and my right leg being immobilized with a plastic, blow-up splint device.

OUT OF THE PLANE

The sequence of events following the arrival of the rescuers is also somewhat blurred in my memory, either from relief of being found and rescued (and not by the Vietcong) or from the shot of morphine I was given, I can only guess. I can remember being half-carried, half-hauled out the airplane door by a number of helping hands and brought to rest on the ground next to the airplane. I know there was some consideration for my leg when I was moved out of the airplane, but I honestly can't remember how this was done, especially since I do remember looking up from the ground and realizing how high a drop it was from the door to the ground. I could see the back of the upside-down airplane above me, with its tail ten or twelve feet above the ground and pointing downward, and the fuselage burrowed into the side of the mountain. Fortunately, I was spared the view of the front of the airplane by trees and shrubs.

I'm not sure how long I laid on the ground outside the aircraft while rescue continued around me. I remember several events clearly. They first took Bob Ray from the aircraft. However, I lost track of Bob after that and did not see him again until the next day at the base camp hospital. Next, from my directions, they found and removed the soldier with the rifle through his stomach, and I heard their discussions of how to save him.

When a Catholic priest arrived at the scene, I received the sacrament of the Last Rites from him. I knew I was not dying, but any help at that time seemed very welcome. The priest assured me of the same thing and gave me very comforting words of solace.

ATTEMPTED AIR RESCUE

What followed was dramatic, tinged with bits of grim humor even under those awful circumstances. By this time, dusk had settled, and there was a tremendous amount of activity going on around me. People and equipment had been brought in (though I don't know how), and chain saws were cutting down the brush and trees surrounding the crash site. Portable generators and light sets had been brought in to illuminate the crash scene. There were plenty of peeking flashlights all around me.

As I lay on the ground, the first helicopter appearing directly over me, I saw the need for clearing the trees. I later learned we had crashed approximately halfway up the mountain, away from the base camp, and on the outer side of the perimeter. They planned to helicopter those with the worst injuries to the base camp hospital as soon as possible a la *M*A*S*H**.[3]

The first helicopter to be brought in was a big Chinook (CH-47). This was a logical choice since it could carry a number of the injured in one flight. From my vantage point looking straight up, I could see the Chinook would never be able to land—just not enough room—and the tree cutting had not progressed to the point where the helicopter could safely hover over the scene and winch the injured aboard. After several attempts, the pilot had to give up, especially after his dual rotor blades had clipped several tree branches. Witnessing this certainly alarmed me. I know I did not want to be killed by a falling helicopter just after I survived a plane crash!

The Chinook was immediately replaced by a Huey, which is smaller, has a single rotor blade with a smaller swing diameter, and can lift out only one injured victim at a time.[4] The Huey maneuvered itself into the tight air space just above me without clipping tree branches. It was able to hover there, forty or fifty feet off the ground, and drop a wire mesh stretcher basket on its winch.

The first person selected to be placed in the stretcher basket was the soldier who had been on the stretcher in the airplane. I don't know why he was selected to be first, possibly because he was now conscious. He was injured again in the plane crash (gash on forehead, broken arm, in addition to his already broken leg), and he might have been in the best condition to withstand the winch ride up to the helicopter door and the flight to the hospital. He was in pain and vociferously protesting being placed in a wire mesh basket stretcher and winched forty to fifty feet to the hovering helicopter. Things became more tense at this point.

The Huey was having difficulty holding its hovering position above us, and as the wire basket stretcher was lifted off the ground, it began to bounce and sway in wide arcs. I could plainly see and hear the distress of the injured soldier in the wire mesh basket over the noise of the hovering helicopter. Despite this, the stretcher basket was winched to within a few feet of the helicopter door, and it looked like the first rescue evacuation would take place. Just at that moment, the winch slipped or failed, and the stretcher with the injured soldier began to drop toward the ground in a set of jerking falls. The cries of the injured soldier became even louder.

As the stretcher came close to the ground, a number of people were there to grab and stabilize it to reduce the impact of any further falling. After some yelling back and forth between those on the ground and the crewman in the helicopter door, it was apparently decided to try again—over the now outraged protests of the injured soldier. Almost instantly, the wire basket started its bobbing and weaving ascent toward the helicopter door. It can only be described as cruel when, once again, within a few feet of the helicopter door, the winch slipped or failed a second time and the stretcher repeated its series of halting, jerking plunges toward the ground.

There was no way to dismiss the distress of the injured soldier this time as he made his way toward the ground. When the stretcher was caught again by the waiting hands on the ground, the soldier had somehow already unstrapped himself from the wire stretcher and, despite a broken arm and leg, found a way to jump from the stretcher to the ground. At that point, he made it very clear to everyone that he might die where he lay, but he was not going up in that #x?#*#* stretcher for a third time! The Huey was waived off. I later learned this soldier did somehow make it to the base hospital and recovered from all his injuries.

By now, the rescuers recognized that airlift out of the crash site by helicopter was not going to be possible. It was completely dark by this time, and a decision was made to man-pack the injured from the crash site to the top of Hon Cong Mountain. At the top of the mountain was a Signal Corps relay station that had a helicopter pad. The plan was to get the injured to the helicopter pad and then airlift them to the base camp hospital at the bottom of the mountain.

UP THE MOUNTAIN

I was given a second shot of morphine, but despite this, I still have a vivid memory of the ordeal of being man-packed up the side of that mountain in a stretcher. The ordeal was equally shared between me and the six to eight men who packed the stretcher. I can remember my arms, chest, and legs being strapped to a standard army canvas field stretcher with belts. I initially wondered why all the precautions, but soon after we set off, I understood.

It was completely dark except for the flashlights the men carried. The climb to the top of the mountain was *very* steep, and most of the time, my stretcher was almost vertical with my head pointed toward the top of the mountain. It seemed to take about an hour before we reached the top.

There was no trail, but, somehow, the stretcher team found their way over the rocks and boulders and around trees and bushes in almost complete darkness. It was all I could do to hang on to the sides of the stretcher. I thought I would fall off a couple of times despite the restraining belts. The jostling and bumping were having their effect on my hip and leg, and I started to feel some serious pain.

The American GI is remarkable in so many ways. He can be unvarnished, honest, and outspoken at any time, and anyone who has had the honor and great pleasure of leading such men would not have it any other way. As the stretcher team carried me up the mountain, I heard plenty of grunting and huffing from the GIs. The men struggling with the stretcher were making every effort to make the haul up the mountain as easy on me as they possibly could. How can I ever forget the forthright exclamation one of them made while maneuvering my stretcher around a rocky point, "Geez, for a little guy, he sure weighs a lot!"

In another instance from a written account describing the ordeal of moving the injured up the mountain, the stretcher team carrying Daniel R. Madden were especially challenged since he had part of his rifle still protruding from his abdomen. Once again, one of the GI rescuers exclaimed aloud in a moment of plain-spoken wonderment why "the doctors had bothered" to rescue this apparently (to him) mortally injured man. From the stretcher, Madden shot back with candor and the finest of GI wit, "(Well), they can't accuse me of not taking my rifle with me, can they?"[5] That "grace under fire" underlay Madden's courage and strong will to live, and certainly sustained him through his complete recovery from this grievous wound.

As we approached the very top of the mountain, the last thirty feet or so were truly vertical. At this point, the rescue parties and stretcher teams had to form a human ladder with a double row of men serving as the ladder rails. Our stretchers then became the rungs of the ladder as each stretcher was lifted up those thirty feet on the outstretched hands and arms of the double row of soldiers. It was a rough ride, and I was in more pain by the time I was carried over the top and placed on the ground inside a canvas tent with the others injured in the crash. I can remember trying to thank my rescuers, but I'm not sure how I sounded or how it came across. I hope to this day that they understood me.

1st Air Cav Communications Center at top of Hon Cong Mountain
(Image from Louis Galanos's collection, used with permission)

CHAPTER 13
2ND SURGICAL HOSPITAL

THE INSIDE OF THE tent was dark with people standing about, and our stretchers were laid out on the floor of the tent. I believe I got my third shot of morphine at this point. I can't remember how long we stayed in the tent, but I do remember a general officer visiting the tent and being briefed on what happened. Despite the poor lighting, I was able to discern his features, and I could not miss the grim expression on his face as he heard the story.

Another example of GI humor took place that continued to carry and sustain us throughout this ordeal. The chaplains had arrived and were attending to the injured in the tent. I was told later by Jordan Brindley that he was also in one of the stretchers nearby, and a chaplain named Lord was bending over to give him encouraging words of solace and comfort. Chaplain Lord knew Jordan from a previous action in the field where the two of them found themselves pinned to the ground next to each other in a firefight with the enemy. Jordan had noticed the name tape on the chaplain's uniform, and he exclaimed the chaplain's name "Lord" out loud. Recognizing the incongruity of the moment, Chaplain Lord quickly assured Jordan, "No, no, I'm not who you think I am!" Chaplain Lord reminded Jordan of that earlier moment they had shared together, and that light moment under these most trying conditions gave Jordan the courage he needed to hang on.

After some time, I was lifted up and placed inside a helicopter and strapped in. I believe it was a Chinook, but I'm not sure, since the morphine was having its effect. I believe I may have hallucinated several times. I vaguely remember being transported and carried to the base camp hospital.

What I remember next is lying on a table and being asked my name, rank, serial number, unit, and where I hurt. Somebody with a clipboard was writing down the information. Then two army female nurses in fatigues started at the collar of my fatigue shirt with scissors and scalpels, and with one on either side of me, they cut off all my clothes very quickly until I was completely naked. They even cut off my jungle boots!

Then, again, with one on either side of me, they checked my head and body over for bumps and bruises, poked my stomach, had me move my arms, etc., until they were satisfied that my only injury was on my right leg. They then wheeled me into a room to x-ray my leg, then wheeled me into an operating room.

Sometime during the exam procedure, I was told my injury was a broken hip and not a broken leg. This is when the doctor told me they were going to give me a spinal and do what is known as a "closed reduction," placing the femur bone back into the hip socket even though the hip socket was broken. I must confess that I was not sure what a "spinal" was all about, but then someone explained the procedure more thoroughly. I was helped into a sitting position, the spinal injection given in the middle of my spinal cord.

They laid me back on the operating table with the glare of the operating room lights in my eyes. I was surrounded by people in operating gowns, hats, and masks. After some low talking and murmuring among the doctors, I can remember my legs being spread apart, one of the doctors climbing on the operating table, placing his right knee between my legs, hovering over me, and explaining what he was going to do. He said he had to grasp my leg and push it back into the hip socket. He warned it might take a while and not to be disturbed by the actions he had to take nor the roughness of the pushing and pulling that would be entailed. Then he started.

The people surrounding me at the upper part of my body held me and steadied me with their hands. I could not feel it, but somehow, I was aware of the doctor placing his left hand along the top of my right leg and his right hand holding my leg just above and inside my knee. He then proceeded to push inward with his left hand and outward with his right hand so that he was essentially pushing my whole leg upward toward my hip socket.

I'm not sure how long this went on, but I believe there were several tries until I, and everyone else in the operating room, heard a very audible, loud "pop." I may have imagined it, but I also seemed to hear a sigh of relief from everyone surrounding me in the operating room. The popping noise was my leg bone going back into the hip socket. The doctor then hopped off the operating table and went on to the next patient.

I was wheeled on a stretcher back to a ward with eight to ten beds along either wall with an aisle in between. I was placed in one of the beds and told to lie perfectly still and not move my right leg. I was told that if I did so and placed any weight on the leg, my leg would pop out of the hip socket again. I believe I was on an IV drip by this time (which could have been started in the operating room, or even in the tent at the top of Hon Cong Mountain—just can't remember).

RECONNECTING

I really began to lose track of time at this point. I talked to the injured soldier in the bed to my left. The patient in the bed to my right was heavily bandaged and casted. He was either unconscious or heavily sedated, and I don't remember ever having a conversation with him. I believe there was another bed beyond his, and then the last bed in my aisle to the right was Bob Ray's. He had already been operated on, and he was recovering from the anesthesia.

Don't ask me how I discovered it was Bob, but I remember yelling down to him to inquire how he was doing. When he answered back, I knew he was OK. Female army nurses came by at intervals, checking my IV drip, changing the bottle, etc. I know I had a visit by my operations sergeant from the division chemical section, and I can remember discussing the extent of my injuries with him. I guess I must have slept some as well.

My stay at the base camp hospital is still fuzzy, except for two incidents. In the first, voices were raised in argument. I glanced to my right and saw Bob trying to get out of his bed, holding his stomach. I believe he actually made it to his feet (with his IV drip in place) and then yelled at a male attendee who I thought was a doctor standing next to the nurse.

Bob said something like, ". . . you had better start treating this nurse better, or I'm going to report you. I'll see that you're court-martialed," or words to that effect. There was a lot of shushing, and then both the doctor and the nurse helping Bob back into his bed.

It was only after we had both recovered that I found out what had happened. From his hospital bed, Bob observed the doctor giving this nurse a bad time. Either it was the effect of the anesthesia or his sense of male honor, but Bob went to the defense of the nurse.

VIET NAM SPECIAL:

Husband and Wife Nurse Team

Newlyweds Bob and Barbara Williams set up housekeeping for the first time in a tent within mortar range of the Viet Cong! The unusual story of this GI and his wife, both Army nurses, is on page 10.

Poughkeepsie Journal, Family Weekly
June 18, 1967

Bob later shared a newspaper clipping which shed some light. The "doctor" and nurse were both nurses, married, and had gained notice in newspaper stories in the States since the wife insisted on following her husband and was assigned to the same base camp hospital. I will never forget the picture of Bob Ray standing by his bed in his hospital gown, one arm holding his stomach, the other steadying the IV drip, and yelling at the "doctor"!

INNOCENCE IS BLISS UNTIL REALITY HITS

The other incident marked the beginning of the real nightmare in this whole plane-crash episode of my life. It all started somewhat innocuously with someone telling me that in order to immobilize my leg so that the current delicate arrangement between my femur and acetabulum would not be disturbed, it would be necessary to place me in a body cast. My medical team explained that I was going to be evacuated through medical channels and transferred while I was in a body cast. This would provide the best assurance that no accidental weight would be placed on the leg and hip socket. The doctors seemed very pleased that a closed reduction was accomplished on the first try, and they were not going to take any chances and have me reinjure the hip by an unfortunate movement of my leg.

I was told that this arrangement would be only temporary until it could be decided what to do to repair my hip. It was all optimism and blue skies for me at this point, and I didn't even ask how long it would be or when this decision would be made. I had survived a crash where an airplane flew into the side of a mountain with no life-threatening injuries. Surely, the minor inconvenience of having my leg immobilized while they moved me about was a small price to pay. Blessed innocence. Little did I know!

The medical technician who wheeled up his gurney (I believe it was the afternoon of the day after the crash) to transport me to the casting room was neither friendly nor unfriendly—just all business. I would later reason that this man knew exactly what he was about to do to me! And the less he got to know me or had to explain to me what he was doing, the easier it was for him (and his conscience) in the long run. Perhaps it was better that way—even for me.

If I knew what I was about to endure for the next six weeks, I probably would have resisted violently. I had only one other cast in my life. During my Firsty (senior) year at West Point, I injured my left knee (torn cartilage) during an "intra-murder" softball game the month before graduation. That had been an inconvenience and a scare of a possible delay in graduation, but it had an upside—I was excused from all the Spring Parades! However, soon after the technician in Vietnam started to cast me, I knew this time was going to be vastly different.

I can remember having to lay flat and perfectly still on some very uncomfortable table. I did not realize how long it would take either. At first, it did not seem so bad, but as the technician wrapped more and more of my body, I began to realize that I was now about to end up in a truly fixed and very uncomfortable position.

The wrapping went around both of my legs, the left leg just below the knee, the right one all the way down to the ankle, and up my body to the top of my chest just below my arm pits. An opening in the body cast was sculptured in my crotch for obvious reasons, but little did I know then how inadequate it was, or just how unnatural. It was bad enough to have both legs wrapped, but then came the ignominy of having a pole cast between my knees in order to fix them in place!

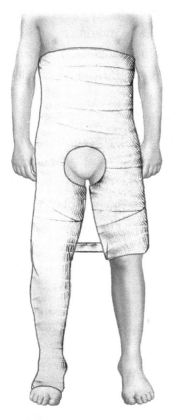

My true immobility and dependency really began to sink in when the plaster casting material began to harden. I might have detected a little of the wry humor the technician was trying to offer when he cut a square opening (approximately two-by-two inches) centered just below my chest. I remember him saying that I would be wanting to look for a wire hanger, straighten it out, and use it as a scratching device—and how proficient I would become with a little practice!

I began then what would become a constant mental exercise for the next six weeks. I had to continuously go through the crash scenario in my mind, recognize how lucky I had been to survive, and rationalize the current state of my discomfort—and

Diagram of spica body cast

dependency. The dependency thing was new for me. I had never been in a position where I had to rely entirely on others for just about everything. When you are in a body cast, there is little that you can do for yourself. You are dependent on others to move you about, feed you, place the bedpan under you, remove it, etc. I hated being dependent on others. The next six weeks had some highs and lows for me, but the constant low was the discomfort of that body cast.

CHAPTER 14
NOTIFYING FOLKS
BACK HOME

AS I WAS RECOVERING at the base hospital at An Khe, the notice of the crash and my injuries were being sent through official channels to my next of kin (Sue and Mom). However, I don't think I can ever explain how two people became aware of the crash through "other" channels. Little did I know that halfway around the world, on the night of 3–4 October 1966, my daughter Susanne (two days shy of her eighth birthday) awoke after midnight and began to sob hysterically.

She fled from her room to the bedroom where my wife, Sue, was sleeping, awakening her mother. Sue tried to calm her and asked her what was wrong. Susanne said, "Something bad has happened to Daddy!"

It took a great deal of comforting to calm her down and get her to go back to sleep with the understanding that it was "just a bad dream." The fourteen-hour time difference made the time she awakened concur with the time and date of the crash.

Surprisingly, my fate was also revealed to a classmate from the Chemical Officer Career Course, Major (retired as a Colonel) Paul Gardner, who was then serving with the 4th Infantry

Division at Pleiku. When Paul heard about my plane crash, he sent me a letter. He described how on the night before my plane crash on October 3, he had a dream about me in which I was in a plane crash and survived. When he heard the details of my actual plane crash occurring on 4 October some time after the fact, he was utterly astonished because it was exactly as he had dreamt about it. Paul himself was later injured in a helicopter crash. This dedicated officer served three tours in Vietnam (two of them voluntary) at the cost of his marriage.

WESTERN UNION

Back at our rental house on Darling Street, Sue awoke on the morning of 6 October. On the same street lived Dr. Reid Appleby and his wife Dawn. The Applebys had recently moved to the neighborhood just after Dr. Appleby's active-duty tour in Vietnam. He was now serving an internship at a nearby hospital. Sue became friends with Dawn when they discovered they shared the same experience of waiting while their husbands were away in Vietnam. Remembering this time, Sue recalls:

I met Dawn one day while putting Susanne on the school bus. Dawn was at home in the day with her son who was the same age as Marly. She found out that Joe was deployed, and she said to me, "You know, I know how to cope with this, so why don't you come have coffee with me every morning when you put Susanne on the school bus?" And I did.

Every morning I would drop off Susanne and go to Dawn's. Marly and their son would play together. She knew how to get all the stations with the news from Vietnam, so she tuned them in for me, and I'd watch and have my cup of coffee and leave to go home.

This one day when I went home, I noticed my neighbors were all out on their doorsteps. The Western Union guy had asked them if they knew where I was. But I didn't know any of them very well, and nobody said anything to me when I arrived home.

So, I went to the mailbox and retrieved a message directing me to "Please call Western Union and a cab driver will deliver the telegram to you." I knew it could not be anything good.

They delivered the telegram. I read it and immediately gathered up Marly and went right back to Dawn's.

Reading the telegram, Dawn finishes and says, "I'm going to call Reid at the hospital."

All the telegram really said was he had been injured, and he is in satisfactory condition, which was far from the truth, but that's okay. I knew he was alive. After hearing the contents of the telegram, Reid told us over the phone, "The war is over for Joe."

Dawn was a very wonderful young woman. Of course, she had been through wondering what was going on over there. From there on in, I just had to wait until I could hear something. But I didn't hear for a good while because they were moving him all around.

They finally got a call to me once he was settled in Japan. Of course, phone call quality was very poor in those days, and there was a time limit. All he really said was, "I'm alive," and "How are the kids?"

I remember, during the call from Japan, that Marly was nearby, eighteen months at the time, and Joe must have said something about having a broken hip. Marly was just beginning to expand her speech, and she started repeating, "Broken hip . . . hop." And she proceeded to dance around singing, "Broken hip . . . hop! Broken hip . . . hop!" Those were some of the few words she could say when Joe got back home.

I had not really read anything else new until Joe started working on the book. I have heard the story of the crash as he always tells it, but I didn't really realize until reading his expanded story about the hospitals and really how bad it could have been—how bad it was. It's a good thing I didn't know it then! But because of the Applebys, I knew a little bit more of what to expect than I would have otherwise. The telegram and the two phone calls did not give me much to go on.

```
951A EDT OCT 06 66 BA064                    Bid Full New
                                           AP    #63-7
SPA035 SYA203 SY WA133  XV GOVT PD FAX WASHINGTON DC 6
728A EDT
MRS SUSANNE T TEDESCHI, DONT PHONE REPORT DLY DONT DLR BETWEEN
10PM AND 6 AM
  41 DARLING ST WARWICK RI
THE SECRETARY OF THE ARMY HAS ASKED ME TO INFORM YOU THAT YOUR
HUSBAND MAJOR JOSEPH R TEDESCHI WAS SLIGHTLY WOUNDED IN VIETNAM
ON 4 OCT 66  HE SUSTAINED A DISLOCATED RIGHT HIP. HE WAS A
PASSENGER ON A MILITARY AIRCRAFT WHICH CRASHED INTO THE SIDE
OF A MOUNTAIN ON APPROACH TO LANDING STRIP. HE WAS TREATED
AT 2ND SURGICAL HOSPITAL, APO SAN FRANCISCO, CALIF 96294 AND
IS BEING HELD FOR FURTHER TREATMENT SINCE HE IS NOT REPEAT
NOT SERIOUSLY WOUNDED NO FURTHER REPORTS WILL BE FURNISHED.
ADDRESS MAIL TO HIM AT THE ABOVE MEDICAL FACILITY
  KENNETH G WICKHAM MAJOR GENERAL USA THE ADJUTANT GENERAL.
```

The telegram both Sue and Mom received

MOM'S CONFUSION

Elsewhere in town, other events were preoccupying my mother on that day. The essential facts are that while I was crashing into a mountain in Vietnam, my brother was in the process of returning from Italy to the US with his new bride. At that time, my mother had been dealing with two very stressful situations. She had one son fighting in Vietnam and the older son in Italy courting and about to marry a girl she had never met. Trying to get my thirty-four-year-old brother hitched, my mother, along with my Uncle Tony, plotted to effect as close as was possible in 1966 an "arranged" marriage with a girl from their village, Fornelli, in the old country.

Their plan worked, and Mike met and fell in love with Ersilia and asked her to marry him—and she accepted! However, the village priest was not about to bless this hasty marriage and allow my brother to take one of his village girls off to the US. After a lot of letter writing and scheming on how to accomplish the wedding civilly in Italy and have a church wedding back in the States, the village priest finally gave in and married them in Italy. After the marriage ceremony, my brother telephoned my mother with the happy news and said he would send her a telegram with the details of their arrival flight home into Logan Airport with his new bride.

Now, I am in no position to judge, but I would say my mother's focus on 6 October 1966 was on the news that her older son had just been married and was about to bring his new bride, whom she had never met, home from Italy to live in the US.

My mother had several relatives and friends in her living room discussing the news of my brother's marriage when the Western Union messenger rang the doorbell and handed her a telegram. I can only imagine the look on the Western Union messenger's face as he passed the telegram to my mother, and she remarked, "Oh good. I've been expecting this. Thank you very much."

The messenger knew it was a telegram from the Department of Defense and that it usually meant sad news for the recipient, though if it had been a notification of death in combat, a US Army officer would have brought the news personally to the next of kin. (Although with the large number of deaths in Vietnam, I was told that even this courtesy was dispensed with during the height of the war.) The news of my being injured in the plane crash did not warrant direct notification, so delivery by Western Union messenger was proper and correct. The same was true for the notification provided to Sue that was taking place just a few miles away and explains why the Western Union messenger left a notice with further directions in the mailbox for direct delivery of the telegram.

The Western Union messenger must have thought he had encountered the most callous mother in the world when my mother then put the telegram in her apron pocket without even reading it! Likely thinking it was the promised telegram from my brother, she could read the details of the flight home later. She was more interested at that point in returning to her friends in the living room and continuing the discussion of Mike's marriage. It was only later when Sue called to inform Grammy of the plane crash and my injury that she finally took the telegram from her apron pocket and read it for the first time.

CHAPTER 15
MEDEVAC

BACK IN AN KHE at the 2nd Surgical Hospital, I was wheeled back to my bed in the ward and thus began my long haul through medical evacuation channels leading eventually to the Chelsea Naval Hospital in Chelsea, Massachusetts. I must have stayed at the base hospital at An Khe for a couple of days, and then I was moved by ambulance to another field hospital at Qui Nohn. I have only the vaguest memory of this trip.

They stacked me with four other stretcher cases in the back of the ambulance. I don't remember how long it took. I can't even remember talking to the guys in the other stretchers—one just above me and two on the other side of the narrow aisle. I believe this began the Darvon or Demerol pills before and during each phase of travel. They are painkillers that also make you drowsy and sleepy. The attending medical corpsmen or the nurses accompanying me on these various legs of my journey administered the medications. After a while, I learned to ask for them as well.

I believe I spent only one night in the ward at Qui Nohn since this was just a staging point for transfer to Clark Air Force Base in the

Philippines. However, I remember being in the middle of the ward this time and having survivors of the crash on both sides of me. One of them was in a body cast as well.

I also remember a dignitary or celebrity (a woman?) come through the ward, exchanging a few words with each of the patients, and promising to call home for us when she returned to the States. I learned more details of the crash from the two survivors next to me. During this stage, I was told that about half the people on the airplane survived the crash (fortunately, the percentage was a bit higher). A large manila envelope carrying my original X-rays accompanied me as well. While at Qui Nohn, they x-rayed my hip again and added that set to the manila envelope. I imagine this was done to ensure that my leg was still in my hip socket.

Trying to recall all these events thirty-two years later, my memories were limited by my vantage point of being constantly on my back and seeing only that which was in the immediate vicinity. There must have been an air base at Qui Nohn, but how I got from the ward to the airplane is forgotten—probably by ambulance.

I vaguely recall the flight from Vietnam to the Philippines. I can remember it was a US Air Force prop plane with stretchers stacked from floor to ceiling of the airplane, and the nurses were now air force flight nurses. All the patients on that flight were immobile stretcher cases. I can remember the solicitous care these nurses gave to each of their transient patients. These wonderful people had the job of getting us to our next destination with the highest degree of safety and comfort.

I don't recall how long the flight took, but it seemed like several hours. From the fog of Darvon and Demerol, I stared at the canvas back of the stretcher above me. I remember how scared I was to be back in an airplane again, but I was resigned that I had no other choice. I had to begin to believe in the comforting presumption that I would never be in a second plane crash!

ENCOUNTER WITH A CLASSY LADY

After landing at Clark Air Force Base, we were transported to a modern base hospital by a blue air force bus that accommodated our stretchers in the now familiar stack. No sharp memories about all this except the realization and recognition of the signs that we were now out of the battle zone, and everything, including the nurses' uniforms, were back to normal white. The overall pace and outlook were clearly becoming "stateside" and away from the war zone. I was placed in a transient ward with about twenty other immobilized patients—the usual ten or so beds along each wall with an aisle in the middle.

I had been placed in the first bed along one of the walls. I can remember being visited by a nurse who did the usual check-in patient profile—temperature, pulse, blood pressure. I remember another set of X-rays being taken and added to my manila envelope. This last set was done by a portable X-ray device that was brought to my bed and the X-rays taken right there in the ward.

I was next visited by someone I thought was yet another nurse. This lady wore what appeared to be a nurse's uniform dress but with an apron. She was pushing a wheeled cart with several metal wash bowls containing warm water. Since I was in the first bed, she started with me and asked if I wanted a bath. We had traveled for what seemed like all day, and I was tired and feeling somewhat travel weary—all this over and above the discomfort I was feeling in that body cast. It had been several days now since I was placed in the cast, and my body and skin beneath the cast were telling me how abnormal this situation really was.

I tried to make light of the situation and told the lady, passing my arm over the body cast, "Whatever is exposed of me, I would be grateful for a bath."

The exposed parts of me outside the body cast were my head, shoulders, and arms, the two-by-two-inch square cut out on my chest, my left leg below my knee, and my right foot. The lady never hesitated and immediately took a washcloth, dipped it in the warm water, soaped it up, and began to wash the exposed upper part of my body. Even under these extraordinary circumstances, it is somewhat embarrassing and awkward to be washed by a stranger—and a woman. If I wondered what I was going to say or how I was going to feel, the lady put me completely at ease.

She immediately began to ask me questions as she washed me. "What's your name? Where are you from? Where were you hurt? How were you hurt? Do you have family? Where are they?" Somewhere in the conversation, she mentioned she had noticed my West Point class ring and asked me what class I had been in. She told me her husband was a West Point graduate as well.

As she spoke, a flash thought went through my mind that this lady was the wife of a West Point graduate who went into the air force after graduation (you could select air force as a career choice back then). He must be stationed at Clark Air Force Base, and she was a Gray Lady volunteering her help with the Red Cross at the base hospital.

Then I asked her, "What is your husband's name? I just might know him. Where is he stationed?"

The next two events happened almost simultaneously. As I asked the last two questions, my eyes glanced over at the little rectangular metal name tag she had pinned to her apron. It said, "WESTMORELAND." This incredible recognition was coming over me just as she was saying, "My name is Kitsy Westmoreland, and my husband is General Westmoreland. He's in Vietnam right now, although he was just here for a short visit and left last night."

As the full recognition hit me, I blurted out, "Mrs. Westmoreland, you do me great honor!"

She replied, never stopping for a second giving me my "bath," "No, no—you give *me* great honor."

The remainder of my bath was spent trying to understand how the wife of the commanding general of US Forces in Vietnam, a four-star general in the US Army, was giving me a bath! In the most unpretentious and straightforward manner, Mrs. Westmoreland explained how she and her two children had tried living in several places while General Westmoreland served in Vietnam, but in these places, and particularly in their last location in Massachusetts, the harassment and ominous phone calls became too much for her, especially as it related to their children. The decision was then made to move the family to the Philippines and to be as close to her husband as she could. He was occasionally able to slip away from Vietnam to visit them, as he did just recently.

After finishing bathing this awe-struck major, Mrs. Westmoreland said she would return and talk to me some more, and then she proceeded to the next bed and asked its occupant whether he would like a bath. And that's the way it went for the next hour or so before she finished her task and really did return and talk to me again. We talked for a few more minutes about families and West Point, and then she left me.

I had watched Kitsy Westmoreland go from bed to bed around that entire ward, and as best as I could observe, she had given a bath to every one of those twenty or so occupants.[6] This was a mixed, transient ward, I later found out. There were no rank or service differences on this ward—just hurting military men, wounded or injured in Vietnam. I remember there being officers and enlisted men—all races, soldiers, sailors, marines, airmen. This was a staging and decision point in the medical evacuation channels out of Vietnam. The seriously ill and wounded would be identified and sent directly home to the United States; the less seriously wounded and injured would be sent to Japan to one of two general hospitals there for treatment and surgery and possible return to Vietnam.

I was told by one of the nurses that Kitsy Westmoreland met this flight every day, and she greeted the wounded and injured coming out of Vietnam just as she did for me—with a warm smile and a bath. For the cynical reader, I want to say that this act was clearly much more than a token or symbolic gesture by the wife of the senior US military officer in Vietnam. This was very hard work that filled a real need, providing comfort and relief to immobilized, wounded, and injured military men coming out of Vietnam. This was the act of a classy lady who matched her feelings and beliefs with actions and example. I doubt that most of the men she bathed and comforted ever knew her name or who she really was.

Years later, I recalled my "bath" with Kitsy Westmoreland in a speech I gave at the West Point Founder's Day Dinner 2009 as the oldest grad attending. (See Appendix C.)

INDOMITABLE SPIRIT

My only other memory of the overnight stay in the transient ward at Clark Air Force Base was less memorable, but it told me a lot about the human spirit and that unique brand of American humor associated with the military. Time takes on a different pace when you are immobilized in a hospital bed. You have too much time to think, and it's very easy to dwell on yourself and the injuries that brought you there.

This was a ward of all immobilized patients, with a variety of casts and slings, reminding me of the last scene in the movie *It's a Mad, Mad, Mad World,* where Spencer Tracy and all his cohorts are in a hospital ward all similarly bandaged, cast, and slung. These were hurting people, and during the supper meal and afterwards, things were very quiet and sedate in the ward. Strangeness of surroundings, strangers in the bed next to you, uncertainty, and even fright were all bearing down on the collective psyche of the men in this ward. A sad, almost melancholy, atmosphere hung in the air. The men knew they would be going separate ways in the morning—some to Japan, some home to the US. It was not a happy moment in time.

Adding to this mood, a nurse came through the ward and said we would be having lights out shortly. Even after the lights were turned off in the ward, I could still make out the rows of beds and their occupants. For the first few minutes after the lights were off, it was deathly quiet. And then, from one of the beds in the middle of the ward, a voice spoke out, breaking the silence, as if finishing the last of his prayers, the speaker mocked, ". . . and God bless the marine corps!" That started it!

From somewhere, a pillow was thrown at the speaker, and then some patients made various catcalls and jeered, and for the next ten minutes—pandemonium! I heard howling and banter, and some genuine laughing. Now we were all at Boy Scout camp on the first night of camp week. There was more razzing, and all the services were equally insulted and praised. Some more pillows were thrown. Things clattered to the floor.

No one came from the nurses' station, although they certainly must have heard the commotion. It finally ran out of momentum and stopped on its own. Just as suddenly, it became quiet again. A pressure valve had been released and everyone seemed to know it. Now it was time to get serious again because we were all in a serious situation. Now it was time to sleep.

I ALWAYS WANTED TO VISIT JAPAN

I was tabbed to go to Japan to see if they could repair my hip with the possibility that I could be returned to duty in Vietnam. I was pleased by this because it told me that my injury could not be that serious or they would be sending me home to the US. I really wanted to complete my thirteen-month tour of combat duty with the 1st Air Cavalry Division since I had only been in Vietnam about three weeks. I had volunteered once to make that God-awful wrench from my family, and I did not want to have to do it again. If I returned to the States, my tour would not have been completed, and I would be subject to another Vietnam tour at a later date. At least, that was the reasoning that buoyed me as the transfer process started again, this time from Clark Air Force Base in the Philippines to Yokota Air Force Base in Japan.

Again, the memories of the travel between stops in the medical evacuation chain all seem to blend together. There was the blue bus to take us to the airfield at Clark; the rows of stacked stretchers; the dedicated flight nurses; the tedium; the pain-killing pills; the now beginning-to-itch body cast that continued to immobilize my body and punish my psyche. I do remember being moved by helicopter from Yokota to the 106th General Hospital at Kishine Barracks in Japan. A click of the remote, and the next scene in my mind is being in a ward at the 106th General Hospital.

This was a bigger ward with quite a few beds against both walls and a much wider aisle in the middle. I was in army channels now, and the nurses and corpsmen were all army folks. The head of the ward was Major Billy, a large blond woman who combined compassion and common sense within a necessary structure of rules and discipline. It was clear who ran the ward and who was boss. The patients were in various stages of repair.

During the three weeks I was there, the people occupying beds in the ward varied. Some were in their last stages of recovery from an operation, mobile, and, in every sense, back to "normal." Others were in the familiar casts and slings, and completely immobilized in their beds—as I was. The newly arrived were at the start of their repair process, usually meaning an operation of some sort. I remember one welcome change. I was placed in an orthopedic bed which had a frame from which a trapeze-like swing was dangled above my chest. This allowed me to reach up and pull my body-casted self off of the bed in sort of a horizontal pull-up.

CHAPTER 16
A LONG THREE WEEKS

DURING THE THREE-WEEK STAY at the 106th General Hospital in Japan, I felt the full spectrum of emotions. The real discomfort I was feeling at this point was from the body cast. Despite my best efforts at washing, I was having more and more problems with skin rashes and itching. The coat hanger could only reach so many places!

Lying around in bed all day and all night was really beginning to wear down on my psyche. I could get some exercise by pulling up on the bar above me, and shortly after I arrived, a hospital physical therapist came to see me with weights, dumbbells, and a strip of cloth.

What was exposed got exercised. My left leg, which was free from the knee down, was exercised with a weight in the strip of cloth from the side of the bed. My arms and shoulders were exercised with the dumbbells. This helped a little. I began to lose my appetite as well. I was leaving more and more of my food on the tray after each meal, and this was noticed by Major Billy. This all had to do with normal bodily functions—which I was never able to resolve until they cut off my body cast just prior to my operation in Boston.

I was attended to by several doctors as soon as I arrived. I received the same treatment I had experienced at each way station along the medical evacuation route. I was getting used to it by now. My manila envelope that had been tucked into my blankets and stretcher, containing medical records and all previous X-rays, was snatched up and filed at the 106th General Hospital.

Once again, another set of X-rays were taken, and I had the usual work up of heart, blood, urine, etc. I had a complete physical exam, testing as much as possible while still in my body cast, conducted by a young doctor who was sort of the ward intern. He returned a couple of days later with all the results of the exam accompanied by an orthopedic doctor. They consulted with me about my injury, its prognosis, and where we stood right now.

They said I had a very serious hip injury that had had a successful "closed reduction" to place the leg bone back in the hip socket without surgery but now required as soon as possible an "open reduction," *i.e.*, surgery to repair that portion of the hip socket that had been broken off the acetabulum (apparently a good-sized piece of the bone).

The doctors could not tell me more at this point about what the operation would entail (pins, screws, rods, etc.). They seemed to indicate that they would know more about what to do once they opened me up. They hinted at the possibility of maybe several operations. But all this was being held up because of a more immediate problem. I had blood in my urine, and the doctors wanted to clear that problem up first before they operated. They did not know whether I had been injured internally in the crash (unlikely since the amount of blood in the urine was microscopic) or whether I had some sort of jungle intestinal infection causing the problem. I was started on a regimen of vitamin C—massive doses several times a day. This was meant to cure my intestinal infection.

THE WAITING GAME

In the meantime, having established a baseline, my urine was checked every day, and when the blood in my urine disappeared, I could expect to have my hip operation right away. A week went by with no progress. Another consultation with the doctors; we'll wait some more. Another week went by, and I still had blood in my urine. I began to see some serious concern by the doctors as they held consultations with me, especially the orthopedist. He explained to me that the operation needed to be done soon or the piece of bone broken away from the acetabulum would start to calcify—and then it would be more problematic to operate. In the meantime, I started my third week in that body cast in that bed in that ward in that hospital in Japan.

I was in the second-to-last bed, and in the bed to my right was Bob Balderson. Of all the patients I got to know in those three weeks, I became most closely attached to Bob. All the others were either transient or so immobile that there was just no occasion for visiting bed to bed. I can remember talking "at a yell" to several people farther down the row to my left who were similarly casted and in slings attached to their orthopedic beds. They all had stories to tell, but mostly we gave each other mutual courage and support to face our pain and discomfort and fears of upcoming surgery. Much of this was done with humor. No one was allowed to get too serious. We all knew when someone was brought back from the operating room after spending some time in recovery. The curtains were drawn around their bed for a while, and all respected that, but once they were drawn back, they became fair game again.

Bob Balderson had been injured by a land mine. It left a lot of shrapnel in his leg, which the surgeons were removing through successive operations. One of the pieces of shrapnel had done something really weird to his ankle, and on several occasions, doctors surrounded his bed with stethoscopes at the ready, all "listening" to the blood flow in his ankle.

From what I could pick up from their conversations, a piece of shrapnel had fused arteries to veins, which would have to be corrected. Bob went through one of his operations while I was there, and I went through the pre-operation worries with him. In turn, he listened to my problems of needing and wanting an operation but being held up in this body cast by blood in my urine.

I'll not forget the closeness and camaraderie of our bedside attachment. Years later, I ran into Bob in the Pentagon. He had recovered from all his wounds, and even his ankle had been restored to some degree of normalcy. Our meeting briefly revived the emotions and feelings we felt at that time. But now we were both restored to health again, and the requisite reserve of well people would only allow us to glance back at a time in our lives when two hurting people really needed each other's support.

The three weeks at the 106th General Hospital were very long for me, yet I can only remember snippets now of how I spent my time. Several incidents remain very vivid. I guess I was beginning to look very wan and pale by this time, and I will never forget the young army nurse, Lieutenant Brumbach, short, dark-haired, and peppy, who showed up at my bedside one of those days with a gurney. She transferred me from the bed to the gurney and informed me we were going outside to get some air. What delight I found in such a simple thing as being left outside in the October sunshine for an hour or so. The weather was pleasant, as I remember, but I needed blankets.

Lieutenant Brumbach did this for me several times more. I wonder if she will ever know how much it did for my morale. Note for nursing schools: Never miss a chance to move your patients outside—especially the bedridden and those in body casts! Bless you, Lieutenant Brumbach.

Among the other morale boosters: I began to receive mail several days after I arrived at the 106th General Hospital. THANK YOU, Armed Forces Postal System. You, too, will probably never know how much you did for my morale. Somehow, you forwarded all my pre-crash mail I should have received in Vietnam and while in transit, and I was caught up in a very short time. Then I started getting post-crash mail directly from home. Somewhere in here there was a bedside phone call to Sue in Rhode Island. Was it the Red Cross who arranged it? I can't remember.

RECOGNITION AND RESOLVE

On one of these waiting days, mail call brought a package of photographs of my eighteen-month-old daughter, Marly. My wife, Sue, was having photographs of my two daughters made (pre-crash) so that I could have them during my thirteen-month tour in Vietnam. I was going to miss over a year of both my daughter's lives, but at least I would have their photographs to sustain me.

When I opened the package, there were a half dozen or so poses of Marly sitting in a blue smock, wearing little white shoes. Her hair was cut short. One of her hands was formed into a little fist. It's very difficult to describe all the emotions I felt just then, but I assure you, I cried. There were tears of incredible joy at seeing these pictures of my child, but these tears were mixed with tears of terrible anguish at the realization that I might never have seen her again. Up to that very moment, I don't think I fully understood the impact and implications of surviving the plane crash.

The photographs of Marly were my catalyst to this fuller understanding. I had been clearly overwhelmed, almost numbed, by events that led me to this hospital bed in Japan. In one instant, it all came into sharp focus for me. I know I cried for a long time, and the feeling would not leave me right away. I know Bob Balderson, Major Billy, and Lieutenant Brumbach all noticed my crying, and when they each tried to probe, all I could do was wave them off for a while. I gradually stopped crying, but I would not let go of the pictures. I couldn't even trust the nightstand next to my bed to store them. The pictures stayed with me in my bed and survived the rest of my journey back to the States, and we now have them in scrapbooks.

After wringing myself out with tears of joy, anguish, and relief, the only antidote I found to console me that day was resolve. In a sense, I have spent the rest of my life resolved to understand why I was one of the survivors of the crash. I know this resolve started that day back there in that hospital bed in Japan. My life was completely changed by this experience. Much of my resolve related to my commitment to my wife and children. Other aspects involved seeking a rational understanding of such an awful event, which I might never completely understand in my lifetime.

ENTERTAINMENT

Certainly not meant to be a morale booster by its proponents, the Sunday afternoon demonstrations by the local Japanese Communist Party outside the hospital proved to be a big boost. I can't exactly explain why this was so, but I know I felt that way, and I detected the same feelings from the others who watched these twenty-minute-long staged and orchestrated demonstrations from the hospital windows each Sunday.

The Communist Party, we were told, had to get permission from the Japanese police to hold the demonstrations. The permission granted an exact starting time and an exact finishing time. Prior to the start time, the demonstrators would begin to gather with their placards in front of the hospital. At precisely the start time, the demonstrators would start waving their placards and shouting, "Yankee, go home! Yankee go home!" Standing nearby were the white-gloved Japanese police with their batons at the ready, sometimes numbering more than the demonstrators.

The demonstration proceeded for precisely twenty minutes. Those of us who could would watch the demonstration from the hospital windows. The bedridden could hear the chanting from their beds. At the finish time, the demonstrators stopped waving their placards, and it became silent again. Any continuation of the demonstration beyond the exact twenty minutes would have brought swift retaliation by the Japanese police.

Perhaps it was the incongruity of the whole situation and scene that boosted my morale. Here was a hospital full of vulnerable, wounded American GIs being demonstrated against by a faction of the Japanese people who were hostile to the American cause and supportive of the Vietcong and the North Vietnamese enemy. What we Americans stood for was their right to demonstrate and express their political beliefs. What our enemies stood for would take away and destroy this right, and yet these Japanese Communists supported the enemies of freedom and demonstrated against us.

The Japanese government and police obviously understood this contradiction very well, and for this reason, the Communists were allowed to demonstrate, but they were very precise about the length and nature of the demonstration each Sunday. What the demonstrators never understood, and could never possibly comprehend, were the loud jeers, yelling, and clapping that came from the hospital at the end of each demonstration. Some of it was expressing mock agreement with the demonstrators on the "Yankee, go home" part, but most of it was an "in your face" reaction by the patients—young Americans, most of whom had no idea what the demonstration was all about, who just did not like being taunted and insulted by any foreign national. Somehow, this whole thing raised my morale.

NEXT STEPS

In my third week at the 106th General Hospital, I had my final consultation with the ward intern and the orthopedist. They were frank and candid with me. They could not clear up the blood in my urine, and they hesitated to operate on me in Japan to repair my hip. I began to suspect that my injury was more severe than I was originally told.

I had been led to believe and expect that I could have surgery in Japan, recuperate, and return to Vietnam to complete my tour of duty. Instead, the doctors were now recommending that I be medevaced back to the States where the facilities and overall services were better for me.

I was feeling a little fear at this point and disappointment that I had yet another leg in my medical evacuation journey to endure before I could start the process all over again to get well. I felt the past three weeks had been wasted. Why was I shipped all the way to Japan to end up confined to a bed for three weeks in a body cast when I could have been sent directly home to the States from the Philippines for treatment? I felt that "my war" was slipping away from me and that my part in it was ending somewhat ingloriously.

I expressed these feelings to the doctors, who in turn told me that I could not return to finish my tour in Vietnam under any circumstances. This led me to ask what the prognosis was on repairing my hip. The orthopedist laid out several options which would be available after they opened me up to determine the extent of my injury.

He talked to me about a fused hip where the upper leg bone (femur) is fused to the hip socket, and one goes through life with a stiff leg and permanent limp. He gave me possibilities of crutches and canes for the rest of my life if things did not go well with the surgery. He also expressed concern as he introduced a new timescale to have the surgery done.

He concluded that I needed to return to the States as soon as possible and have the operation or calcification of the bones was certain to take place. Finally, he told me that I would never have "a mountain-climbing hip" again! I'll never forget that description!

I finally had to accept that I was being told that my war was over. I needed to return to the States to have my operation with some degree of urgency. As the final coup de grace, Christmas was coming, and the policy was to get as many patients home as soon as possible.

CHAPTER 17
HOME BY CHRISTMAS

ARRANGEMENTS WERE MADE TO ship me back to the States to the nearest military general hospital. I was initially given two choices: Newport, Rhode Island or Chelsea, Massachusetts. My list was narrowed to one (Chelsea Naval Hospital) when it was determined that the Newport Naval Hospital did not have the orthopedic facilities to handle my case. My memory is, again, of the gurney coming to my bedside, two (or more) people lifting me off the bed and onto the gurney, and wheeling me out of the ward of the 106th General Hospital.

It may sound crazy, but I got emotional then, too. Leaving Bob Balderson, Major Billy, Lieutenant Brumbach and all the others to whom I had become amazingly attached in three weeks was enough of a wrench for me in my then vulnerable state of mind. I can't remember how I got from the 106th General Hospital to Yokota Air Force Base. I do remember spending one night at the Yokota base hospital—in a room all by myself. Except for a ward nurse coming in and checking on me, I was quite alone and feeling mighty blue.

THE FLIGHT HOME

My next memory is an ambulance taking me to the airstrip and being loaded through the down ramp of a big C-141. It seemed we waited a long time before all the patients arrived and were placed in stretchers (three tiers high, with a double row along the middle and a single row on either side) in the cavernous fuselage of the C-141. I remember being in a center row stretcher on the bottom of a three-stretcher tier. I began to feel complete helplessness in that body cast again. Then there was the issue of bivalving the body cast.

It seems that the medical evacuation people learned a hard lesson in the Korean War. Patients with casts that had been evacuated via airplane had their limbs swell and cut off blood circulation resulting in serious consequences. The air force now had a rule that all casts must be split (bivalved) before any flight to prevent such injuries happening again. I had had my body cast bivalved somewhere along the line. However, other patients being brought aboard the C-141 had not, and most of the time it took to load the aircraft was taken up by a medical corpsman with a portable cutting tool cutting a seam in each cast.

I was feeling some fear of flying, and when the airplane was finally loaded and we prepared to take off, I became keenly aware and sensitive to the noise and whine of the four jet engines on the aircraft. From takeoff to the eventual landing, my ear was attuned to the sound of those engines. Somewhere along the line (perhaps due to the painkillers that I began taking again), I became convinced that the airplane was going to crash, especially over the ocean.

I began to formulate my plan. If the airplane went down in the ocean, broken hip or not, I was going to tear off that body cast so that I had a chance of surviving. I know I began to work on the seams of the split body cast, and by the time we landed, they were all pretty well loosened.

I can't remember the length of the flight, but from Japan to Andrews Air Force Base in Maryland, non-stop, must have been at least twelve to fourteen hours. I can't remember eating or sleeping (though I must have)—only the whine of those jet engines and feeling very uncomfortable and cold, despite being wrapped in blankets.

We were attended to by air force flight nurses who did their usual superb job working with the patients. My most vivid memory is that of a very badly wounded soldier in a Stryker frame. From where I lay in my stretcher, he was somewhere to my right front. I may have seen him in the Stryker frame from my stretcher, and my mind wants me to forget what I saw. Or, I only imagined that I was able to see him, and my mind filled in the details. What I do know for certain was that I could hear him almost constantly groaning in pain and discomfort.

I have this picture in my mind of the soldier strapped to this Stryker frame. The soldier, completely immobile including his head and neck, is regularly rotated by the nurses 180 degrees in the Stryker frame, so that at times he is spread-eagle facing the floor, and when rotated, he is spread-eagle facing the ceiling. This procedure is followed when people have serious spinal injuries and must be moved. The flight nurses seemed to be spending much time with him. I guess I'll never know what happened to him. If I was uncomfortable on this trip, I can only imagine what his return home was like.

WELCOME HOME

My next memory is that of landing at Andrews Air Force Base. I believe it was dark when we arrived. They placed me in an ambulance along with five other patients for transfer to the base hospital. The most extraordinary event occurred then, and one that I will always remember in detail because of the emotions I was feeling at that moment—some of which included the terrible anguish I was feeling about the Vietnam War. (Much of the deception and betrayal I later came to feel about the war were sorted out for me in the book *Dereliction of Duty* by H. R. McMaster, an insightful book of President Johnson's deceit and betrayal of the US Armed Forces and the public during the period just before and after the 1964 election.)

An army full colonel stepped into the ambulance, introduced himself, and in a very sincere voice told us he was the personal representative of President Johnson. He said it was his duty to meet every returning member of the armed forces on these medical evacuation flights and to thank each injured and wounded soldier on behalf of President Johnson and the American public. He thanked us for the sacrifice that we had made in the cause of freedom and assured us that our pain and suffering were not in vain. He shook each of our hands and said "thank you" most sincerely. I had absolutely no reason to doubt the sincerity of this man and the message he gave me at that time.

I was thirty-two years old. I had been pursuing my military career, had volunteered to go to Vietnam, and believed what we were doing was right. I was disappointed I could not get my hip repaired in Japan and get back to the war. At that point, I was more frightened than disappointed that a bad hip injury had the potential to end my military career. I was back on American soil with the prospect of seeing my family again very soon. With serious surgery imminently facing me, the enormity of having survived an airplane crash was never far from my stream of consciousness. Tired and dirty, I felt very, very vulnerable.

The colonel's words and handshake hit me like a bomb. Emotions erupted, and I began to sob. I'll never deny the sincerity of that moment and the performance of that colonel's duty. It took another thirty-two years to realize how badly I, and so many others, had been deceived by Johnson and other high-ranking government officials. I'll always remember and cherish that moment, but today, it is tarnished by what I've come to understand of the betrayal of the American Armed Forces in Vietnam.

My next flash of memory comes from a private room in the base hospital at Andrews, nurses in white uniforms looking after me, and two very sweet Gray Ladies who could not do enough for me. There wasn't too much anyone could do for me at that point except try to make me comfortable. The blankety-blank body cast was just getting worse—I was really itching and feeling dirty all over. Once again, I was at a transition point. I was told I would be shipped out the next day on a medical evacuation flight to Boston (Hanscom Air Force Base) and then proceed to Chelsea Naval Hospital by ambulance. I remember, too, a telephone being wheeled by my bedside and my making a call to Sue to tell her that I had arrived in the US safely and the details of my medevac plans. Sue said she would be there to greet me when I arrived at Chelsea Naval Hospital. I don't need to tell you what that did for my morale!

My memory of the medevac flight to Boston is fairly clear. It was a twin-engine prop airplane, not much bigger than the C-7 Caribou. There was room for several stretchers and seats for ambulatory patients. I believe we had several other patients on board, but for the life of me, I don't exactly remember. There was the flight nurse, again, who could not do much for me except to make me as comfortable as possible.

We did not fly very high, perhaps 10,000 feet, and I can remember being able to see out a window and enjoying the fall foliage below. Likely flying over Maryland, Delaware, and New Jersey, how beautiful the landscape and colors looked to me. We made a stop at Bennett Field in New York, either to let someone off or take on another patient. I took in the New York City skyline as we landed and took off.

We landed at Hanscom Air Force Base where two navy corpsmen met us and placed me on a steel gurney to wheel me from the airplane to a waiting ambulance, grayish white with US Navy markings, a Cadillac model. I next remember being in the back of the ambulance as the two corpsmen sat in the front, all alone and looking out the windows of the ambulance as we drove through the streets of Boston and Chelsea.

I carried along my medical records and X-rays with me in that familiar large manila envelope in the ambulance. The two corpsmen were not particularly talkative. This was 1966, and I suspect, this "run" was fairly routine for them by now—just another injured guy coming back from Vietnam. I seemed to recall, too, it was Sunday, and I wondered how Sue would get from Rhode Island to Chelsea to meet me. I was feeling a bit lonely and sad, and except for knowing that I would be seeing Sue and my girls soon, I guess I was not feeling too good about my homecoming. This was not at all how I imagined it would be.

"GROUNDED" AT CHELSEA

It was around 1600 by the time the ambulance arrived at Chelsea Naval Hospital. From my horizontal position, all I can remember is what looked like a very old brick building. The ambulance drove up to the emergency entrance, and I was transferred to a canvas stretcher. I next remember a discussion bordering on an argument between the two corpsmen. They could not decide whether I should go to the Orthopedic Ward or the Officers' Ward. My injury would suggest the Orthopedic Ward where they had the right kind of beds with frames, etc. But since I was an officer, I should be placed in the Officers' Ward, despite the fact that one of the corpsmen was sure they had no orthopedic beds in that ward.

I don't remember hearing the end of the argument or being told what decision was made. I was aware and sensitive to other points of confusion—like where I should be registered upon entering the hospital. I know it was a Sunday afternoon, and things might have been a little slack and maybe not opportune to bring in a patient in a body cast on a stretcher from Vietnam (an army major to a navy hospital at that!), but things began to get slapstick at this point.

The next thing I knew, these two corpsmen placed me in a stretcher on the floor directly beneath a very high desk (or so it seemed in my low, horizontal position). The desk reminded me of a police sergeant's desk at some old precinct where one got "booked." I lay there for a while, and I don't remember what came exactly next—either the grand reunion with my mother and Sue, or the head peering over the high desk at me and yelling questions at me like: "What's your name, address, phone number?" Perhaps they both happened simultaneously, which is closer to my memory of that happy, humorous, almost burlesque and emotionally-charged scene.

I'll describe what I can of that grand reunion. I can remember lying there on this canvas stretcher, a couple of inches off the floor in a body cast and a little bewildered by now by the entrance procedures to the Chelsea Naval Hospital. I must have had a blanket over me, but not much else on but that body cast. I can remember looking up and suddenly seeing my mother standing there looking down at me, and without hesitation, she knelt on the floor next to me and gave me a big, warm hug. I remember her saying, "My son, my son—are you all right?" I next remember seeing Sue in the vertical position next to me, and she was soon kneeling down on the floor giving me an embrace. I can remember one of them saying how "green" I looked! (It's remarkable to me, but it had been about four weeks since the airplane crash, and I didn't have the faintest memory of how I shaved during that time, or whether I ever got a haircut. I can remember Red Cross kits with toilet articles, so I must have shaved and brushed my teeth! I was given sponge baths by orderlies and nurses. I just don't remember looking into a mirror and seeing myself in terms of needing a haircut or shave, or whether my complexion was "green.")

The other half of this incongruous scene was answering the long list of administrative questions from this face and voice which would peer over the top of the high desk, yell down a question, and I would yell back my response from a few inches off the floor. The head would disappear behind the desk to record the answer, and then reappear with the next question. I might have been a guy who wandered in from the street looking for hospital admittance! Somehow, the grand reunion and the admittance registration ended, and then they wheeled me into a four-person room in the Officers' Ward. Obviously, that argument won over, but I noticed the bed was not an orthopedic bed! A few days later, an orthopedic bed was brought to the Officers' Ward for my use.

COMFORTS OF HOME

Sue stayed with me throughout this time. She joined me after I was set up in the Officers' Ward. She had taken a room in nearby Chelsea, which she found through the Red Cross. At the time Sue was rooming in Chelsea, the "Boston Strangler" had not yet been apprehended. The realization of the danger this involved for Sue did not occur to us until much later when the notoriety of this serial killer had been made known.

My mother was also nearby but must have returned home to Rhode Island that night. I seem to recall that Susanne and Marly did not see me the day I arrived but visited me shortly thereafter. When Susanne and Marly were led into the ward, we had a joyous reunion. Susanne was eight years old then, and I can remember how hesitant she was to come into my room and approach my bed. How frightening it must have been for her. For me, I had the greatest joy and peace of mind knowing that I was back with my family again.

I recall one incident that first night. Sue asked me if I wanted anything special to eat, and she would get it for me. I can't imagine how I came up with clam cakes (boy from Rhode Island), but that's what I asked for. Sue somehow obtained a brown paper sack of greasy clam cakes, and by the time they reached my bed, they had gotten cold. I wolfed them down, cold and greasy, and after a while, nausea brought them back up!

CHAPTER 18
DOWN TO BUSINESS

I WAS MOST FORTUNATE to be assigned an outstanding orthopedic surgeon to handle my case. Dr. Dawkins, Commander in the US Navy Medical Department, paid his first visit to me shortly after I arrived, and he game-planned his approach for me. He told me he planned to connect the piece of bone that was broken loose back to the acetabulum with pins.

Before he would schedule the surgery, he ordered yet another complete set of stereoscopic X-rays to be taken (these were the days before CAT scans and MRIs). He planned to discuss the X-rays and consult with other surgeons at the orthopedic department at nearby Massachusetts General Hospital to devise the best approach to the open reduction surgery. Once all this took place, the surgery would be scheduled for early November, about six weeks after the plane crash. I was beginning to feel more comfortable with my situation and grateful that I was in good and competent hands.

Shortly thereafter, a young navy doctor accompanied me to the X-ray room to take the stereoscopic X-rays. I'm unsure if he was an orthopedic intern or a resident doctor. It was his job to position me for each of a large number of X-rays that had to be taken in order to obtain the stereoscopic picture that Dr. Dawkins wanted. (In the pre-MRI days, they would create the effect of 3D by showing two slightly offset images separately to each eye of the viewer. Both images are of the same scene or object but from a slightly different angle or perspective.) In the chat that took place while this was going on, the doctor indicated that he had just returned from Vietnam himself. He asked me about my injury, how it happened, etc. I relayed my story and gave him an account of my journey through the medical evacuation channels, how I ended up in Japan for three weeks and then had to be sent stateside because of the blood in my urine.

The doctor then exclaimed, "You mean they sent you all the way back here to the States without operating on you? That would never have happened if you were my patient. Your case is too interesting, and I would have performed the surgery in Japan just to get the medical experience."

To which I replied, "You mean you would have kept me in Japan to have the operation just so you could get operating room experience?"

He answered, "Yep. You know how it is. That's show biz!" Once again, I experienced this sense of "Was I lucky or was Someone up there looking out for me?"

HOSPITAL ANTICS

An active-duty air force pilot was in the ward across the hall after having surgery for a knee problem. In the operating room, the anesthesia mask had been placed over his mouth and nose just prior to the operation. As a trained pilot familiar with wearing oxygen masks while in flight, he was conditioned to let the mask assist his breathing so he was not breathing in the anesthetic. Consequently, the anesthesiologist was having problems getting the pilot to "go under."

The anesthesiologist was forced to place a tube down his throat in order to administer the anesthesia, which irritated the pilot's throat.

As he began to recover from the operation, he began to hiccup because of the irritation in his throat. During the first day of his hiccups, everyone considered it a somewhat humorous situation, but by the second and third day of steady hiccupping, the pilot had the hospital staff very worried. They knew they had to stop the hiccupping because steady hiccupping for extended periods of time can apparently lead to serious complications.

The next day was both intense and humorous as various "cures" were tried to stop the hiccups. Many were tried, but none were successful. Finally, one of the nurses tried an "old wives'" cure which consisted of drinking a shot of whiskey (brand unspecified) and then placing a paper bag over the head and breathing rapidly and deeply. To the amazement of all (except for the nurse who suggested it), the cure worked, and the hiccups stopped, greatly relieving the pilot and all of us who heard him hiccupping throughout the day and night for several days.

Obtaining the shot of whiskey was no problem on the officer's ward. To my surprise and delight, I was asked if I wanted a daily "ration" when I was interviewed on entering the hospital. I was a little confused by the question, but as it turns out, I was entitled to a daily "ration" of whiskey by naval custom. I was so surprised by the question that I initially declined the entitlement. However, all of the navy officers on the ward were familiar with the custom, and they did not decline, leading to some interesting problems.

One of the patients in the Officers' Ward was a young navy doctor, a cardiologist, who had suffered two fractured heels. The story told on the ward was that he was late in returning from shore leave, and in the classic manner of those who try to join the ship as it is pulling away from the dock, he apparently jumped from the dock onto the steel-plated deck of the ship, breaking the bones in both his heels. Having both heels in casts required him to move about by wheelchair. Since he was a doctor, he was also helping out with some of the cardiology patients on the ward. A rather bland story up to this point, except that this young doctor had an eye and a hand for the nurses—and he liked to drink! I believe the nurses could hold their own against this young doctor, but the addition of alcohol made him especially bold and boisterous. On the evening in question, this doctor had managed to use up his daily "ration" plus a few others, which he conveniently prescribed to himself or scrounged from others.

Scenes of pure slapstick comedy followed in which the young doctor is seen racing down the hallway in his wheelchair chasing several nurses heard to be either giggling or screaming. We were told later the young doctor had managed to corral one of the nurses in a supply closet, apparently one of the screamers, and held her there against her will. Suffice to say, the incident brought swift repercussions. The "rations" were stopped, and the young doctor was reprimanded for his behavior. Things were quieter after that, but I think everyone secretly missed the antics of this character doctor.

ANOTHER ARMY GUY

After several days in the hospital, I became aware of another army officer patient in a room somewhere down the hall. I first knew about him when I heard someone moaning, yelling, and shouting. The noise was somewhat continuous throughout the day and, unfortunately, at night as well. When I inquired about the commotion, I was told that an army lieutenant had been brought in with a very bad leg injury from stepping on a mine in Vietnam. He apparently was in great pain, and they were trying to stabilize his situation before they operated on him. Giving the orderlies quite a bit of trouble, he had to be isolated in a private room because of his constant moaning and overall disposition. I was told that he was feeling very sorry for himself, which added considerable burden to the hospital staff.

From my recent experience in the 106th General Hospital in Japan, I found this attitude difficult to understand. We had people in the 106th who were injured as badly or even worse than this man, and although people moaned in pain, they did not add to their misery by giving the hospital staff a bad time or by feeling sorry for themselves. As I wrote earlier, the other patients just would not permit it, and anyone feeling bad or blue always got some words of encouragement from his fellow patients. I can't remember exactly how it came about, but I suggested to an orderly that some of the lieutenant's problems might be caused by his isolation. A few days later, the bed to my right became empty, and the lieutenant, another Bob, was moved in next to me.

SHARED MISERY

Things started out slow with Bob. He clearly did not want to be moved into a four-bed room. He initially had the curtains around his bed drawn, and the moaning continued as before. But after a while, the routine of the hospital ward began to force the curtains to be drawn back. I was too obvious and evident to Bob, and he was compelled to acknowledge my presence in the bed next to him. I was still in the body cast at this time, and I may have presented a picture of someone in as bad a situation as his. After introductions, we exchanged stories, and just that seemed to be of some help. I think just talking about what happened to him to another army guy was a beginning. It is amazing the amount of small banter that can be exchanged between two people lying flat on their backs in a hospital ward.

I began to be concerned about what might happen when night came. Our talking had really preempted Bob's inclination to moan, although I could see that the pain he was feeling was very real. I feared Bob would revert to his previous behavior and keep me and the other two people in the room awake all night. I stayed up late that night talking to Bob or, more correctly, listening to Bob for a long time. It became clear this young man was very worried about his future.

He was from the Boston area, had gone to college there, and was in the army on an ROTC commission. The prognosis for his leg and particularly his knee was not very good. He was being told that he would likely end up with a fused knee and would have to go through the rest of his life with a limp and a cane. This is hard news for a young man to take.

I was able to tell Bob that I had also been told that a limp and a fused leg was one of the possibilities facing me. Finding he was not alone with this prospect seemed to help. Bob talked about going to law school and becoming a lawyer as his father had done after World War II on the GI Bill.

Whether from sheer exhaustion or from talking ourselves out, we both fell asleep, and as far as I knew, Bob did not make any disturbances that first night nor any of the following nights he was in the hospital. The next day, Bob was visited by his family—his father, mother, and younger brother. When his father entered the room, one could not help but notice the Silver Star lapel decoration, the cane, and decided limp of his right leg.

IN THE FAMILY

After the family visit, Bob told me his father had been injured in World War II by a land mine and that he was going through life with the limp and cane, something Bob would now inherit. Before he left the hospital, his nomination for the Silver Star had been approved, and now the father-son duality was complete. I'll bet that Bob became a damn fine lawyer, too. I lost track of Bob after he left the hospital, so I'm not able to verify his future, but I would bet my bottom dollar on it.

Chelsea Naval Hospital was the oldest navy hospital and in continuous service since the Civil War. It has since been closed, and probably for good reasons. The monstrosity of old brick looked more like a factory than a hospital. During my stay, it clearly showed the strain of its age. During several rainstorms, the roof leaked badly, and I have memories of numerous water buckets and pans (some bed pans too) being used to capture the water leaks around the hospital. However, the condition of the building was no reflection of the hospital staff. I was greatly impressed by all the doctors, nurses, and corpsmen and will forever be grateful for the outstanding manner in which they looked after me and helped me through this most difficult time of my life.

BRINGING IT ALL TOGETHER

The day of the operation on my hip finally arrived. On the night before the operation, my surgeon, Dr. Dawkins, provided me with a complete description of what he planned to do. Before he started, I told him I had one request. If I promised to be real still and not move, could he avoid placing me back in a body cast after the operation? To my great relief, he said he had no plans to put me back in a body cast. Instead, I would be placed in a sling contraption which would elevate my hip and leg and would give me much more flexibility in movement. He also said he would be inserting two fairly large size screws made of molybdenum, beryllium, and stainless steel through the piece of bone broken loose and literally screw it to the main acetabulum. He said the surgery would be more "mechanical" than "surgical."

Following Dr. Dawkins, the anesthesiologist came in and briefed me on the procedures he would use. He said it would be a rather lengthy operation and that he would give me a spinal and only keep me partially anesthetized during the operation. Then came the visit I had been really looking forward to: the orderly came in with a scalpel and began to cut me out of the body cast. I can't begin to describe the feeling of relief after the last wrapping came off. I was immediately given a chance to bathe with the help of the orderly who also shaved and prepared the surgical area. I was quite surprised by the amount my leg muscles had atrophied in just six weeks.

The anesthesiologist was true to his word. I remember the spinal the next morning and the anesthesia mask administering sodium pentothal, which he used to keep me in and out of consciousness. I glanced at the clock on the operating room wall to measure my time in the operating room. It seemed it was over five hours before I remember being wheeled into the recovery room.

CHAPTER 19
THE LONG ROAD TO RECOVERY

RECOVERY WAS SOMEWHAT NORMAL. The sling in which my leg was placed was tolerable, but compared to the body cast, it actually felt comfortable. When Dr. Dawkins visited me after the operation, he claimed the surgery was a success but that the long-term prognosis was problematic. Much would depend on how my hip and leg recovered and how successful I would be in physical therapy.

Dr. Dawkins also told me that, when inserting the screws, he had bruised my sciatic nerve and that there was a possibility of a "drop foot" in my right foot as a result. Time would tell. (Note: I did end up with a drop foot syndrome which was only painful as the bruised nerve was healing.)

For the first week after the operation, I could not bear to have anything touch the toes on my right foot. This made sleeping difficult, and Sue had to rig a little "tent" over my feet while I slept. In the long term, my right foot "drops" so that I occasionally trip over door sills when my foot does not raise high enough. I also can hear the "slap" of my right foot when I walk down a long corridor. No big deal—a small price to pay for a successful operation. I will always be grateful to Dr. Dawkins and all the staff at the Chelsea Naval Hospital for giving me back my hip and allowing me to walk normally again.

I have never "climbed a mountain" with my hip, but I think I could if the mountain were not too high or steep! The two pins have stayed with me for the rest of my life. After all these years, I have only slight twinges of discomfort with the hip. Dr. Dawkins indicated that there would be long-term prospects for arthritis in this hip, which lately I am beginning to feel. I have tested and challenged my hip for all these years, and it has held up well. I have been a frequent jogger (at one point I would have even called myself a runner), and the hip has survived all that pounding.

The remainder of my stay at the Chelsea Naval Hospital was somewhat routine. After recovery came healing, and then physical therapy. I worked hard with my rock-in-a-sock to begin getting my leg muscles back in shape. I started with crutches and after two to three months eventually moved to a cane. It was almost a year before I got rid of the cane.

Just before Christmas 1966, I started making home visits to nearby Rhode Island. This became a little tricky with the crutches and some sort of soft cast which prevented my right leg from bending. Someone drove me home for the first few visits. After that, I decided to drive myself, which, as I look back on it, was completely insane! If I were ever stopped by a policeman, I would have no excuse for driving in my condition.

On one occasion, I made the visit home by coach bus. Sue accompanied me, and I remember an embarrassing situation which occurred on this bus ride to Rhode Island. It was snowing, and snowplows and street sanders were doing their work. As the bus went along one stretch of the highway, it passed a sander throwing sand, some of which sprayed along the side of the bus as we passed it. The sound of the sand hitting the side of the bus must have triggered in my mind the sound of the airplane scraping the tree limbs just before the crash, and I instinctively doubled over in my bus seat and went into a "crash" position. In the process, my arm went out, and I knocked the hat off the man sitting in the seat in front of us. It was a very awkward moment when the man turned around to stare at me while I was in the doubled-over position. I can't remember how Sue and I talked our way through it, but it seemed to pass without too much fuss.

FIT FOR DUTY

As I started making progress in recovery, the army moved in again, and they wanted to know from the army liaison at the hospital what my status for duty would be. The hospital gave me a temporary "fit for duty" with restrictions and the proviso that I be evaluated by an army Medical Evaluation Board after one year. My Washington military personnel section also began to inquire about my next assignment. In order to be near Walter Reed Hospital for my medical board, I was assigned to the headquarters of the Army Materiel Command, then located in what is now the parking lot of Washington National Airport.

A DEGREE OF NORMALCY

The new assignment, and our next move, came in around February or March of 1967. We packed up our household after just six months, took Susanne out of school again, and moved from Rhode Island to a rental house in Arlington, Virginia.

After the long period of injury, treatment, and recovery, it felt great just being active again, although I was somewhat hampered by crutches and eventually a cane. I was determined to return my life, and the life of my family, back to a degree of normalcy. However, my attempts were seriously challenged by the tumultuous events going on at that time. The war protests, the assassination of Dr. Martin

Luther King, Jr., armed troops with fixed bayonets on the street corners of Arlington, black smoke rising behind the silhouette of the Capitol Building—all this chaos worked against normalcy. Despite the current events, the next two years in Arlington are remembered as one of the happiest times of our family life.

Our concern with our daughter Susanne's schooling was also happily resolved in those two years. She had a serious setback following the tumultuous transition from Alabama to Rhode Island. Susanne started school in Aberdeen, Maryland, attending kindergarten on post at Aberdeen Proving Ground, then first grade and half of second grade at St. Joan of Arc School. Due to my training at Chemical School, she finished the second half of second grade at a private Catholic school in Alabama.

By the time of my departure for Vietnam, she was ready to start third grade in a new school system in Rhode Island. The differences in school systems and standards were just too wide. Susanne was clearly not ready for third-grade work there. The teachers recognized this, and shortly after I left, they recommended Susanne start again in second grade. Along with the strangeness and the newness of yet another school, Susanne's biggest problem in school was clearly missing me.

My going to Vietnam away from my family had caused yet another "casualty" that will never make the statistics of that war. I wonder, how many other kids were impacted by their father's absence during that war?

To Susanne's great credit, she eventually recovered very well from this academic setback. After moving to Arlington, Susanne continued in second grade for the remainder of that 1966–67 school year and for the ensuing third and fourth grades as well. A marvelous teacher at Barcroft School inspired her and gave her back the confidence that she had lost. From then on, there was no looking back. She continued her education at Ft. Leavenworth, Kansas (1969–70), and then on to Salisbury, England, where she spent the next two years (1970–72) at a private Catholic school called La Retraite. Susanne experienced two more school systems before she graduated from high school in Annandale, Virginia. She attended Mary Washington College, graduating in 1981.

Sometime during 1967, my wife Sue wrote a letter to Kitsy Westmoreland, thanking her for giving me a "bath" at Clark AFB. We were living just south of Fort Myer in Arlington where the Westmorelands were living in the assigned quarters for the Army Chief of Staff. We were practically neighbors! About a year later, Kitsy Westmoreland answered Sue with a note that just continued to reflect her elegance and her feelings about the Vietnam War and the soldiers involved.

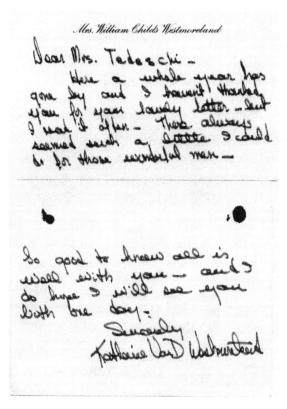

A note Mrs. Westmoreland sent to my wife when Sue thanked her for her care in the Philipines. Another indicator of her concern for all of the Army family.

I continued to be closely involved in the Vietnam War throughout my new assignment with the Army Materiel Command. I initially worked on explosive tunnel destruction systems and new ways to employ agent CS (tear gas). In the latter part of my assignment, I was responsible for monitoring the ENSURE Program (Expedited Non-Standard Urgent Requirement for Equipment). This was a novel approach to getting much needed items to Vietnam without the usual rigorous, long-term approach to developing items for army use.

We acquired and sent sniper rifles, snake bite kits, amphibious boats, and a wide assortment of off-the-shelf equipment to Vietnam for evaluation and use. We had great success with this program. The reports coming back from Vietnam were very satisfying, and I felt I was still contributing something to the success of our troops at war.

THE DAY OF THE MEDICAL BOARD

For the remainder of 1967, I made steady recovery, weaned myself off the crutches and cane, and even began taking small jogs around the neighborhood. As the end of the year approached, it was time for the Medical Board at Walter Reed Hospital. This milestone filled me with dread since it had some possibility of ending my military career after investing ten years in the army. I pictured in my mind a semi-circular table with a Board of Doctors behind it, with all my medical records in front of them, waiting to decide my future. My imagination even placed crossed swords and a burning candle on the table.

The appointed day arrived, and I put on my best Class A uniform and drove to Walter Reed. My imagination really failed me, because as it turned out, I saw a very busy doctor (major) who was obviously overwhelmed along with everyone else with the Vietnam patient load impacting Walter Reed Hospital in late 1967. He sat at a cluttered desk in a small office. He picked up my medical records from the top of a pile and quickly reviewed them. He asked me how I was feeling and then asked me to do a few motions with my leg and hip—which I did.

He then grunted and asked me, "Well, what do you want?"

I was a little stunned by his question, and I had to ask him, "What do you mean?"

He answered, "Do you want in or out?"

It finally dawned on me that he was asking me if I wanted out of the army on the basis of a medical discharge, which would have meant a disability of some sort. I could only surmise that my medical case was such that it could have gone either way, and this doctor (my total "medical board") was willing to support either decision on my part. He must have also experienced other recent cases where the patients were looking for any reason to get a medical discharge at the height of the Vietnam War.

I then explained to the doctor that I was a career army officer, and I wanted as clean a bill of health as he could give me to pursue the remainder of my career. I didn't want my medical record to impede it.

I got the distinct impression that this surprised the doctor, who grunted again, made a mark on one of the papers in front of him, shook my hand and said, "OK, you're fit for duty. However, I wouldn't go jumping out of airplanes too soon!"

That was it . . . the end of this whole ordeal! Approximately a year and a half had gone by since I was in that Caribou that flew into the side of Hon Cong Mountain in Vietnam. This whole episode of my life was finally over to be tucked neatly away in a stack of official files. The only marks now left to remind me were the large scar on my back side where they did the surgery, the two Phillips-head screws holding my hip together, a drop foot which caused me to stumble now and then . . . and a whole lot of memories.

PART 3
A LIFE EXAMINED

CHAPTER 20
AFTERMATH

". . . Career favorites: Army sponsored advanced schooling at Iowa State University, exchange officer with the British Army at their Defence NBC School, several Washington/Pentagon assignments, [and being the] Commander/Director of the Foreign Science and Technology Center in Charlottesville, VA . . ."

I LIVED WITH THESE memories for the remainder of my military career (recorded in Appendix C) and for the rest of my life. I had a full and satisfying career as an army officer with some interesting and challenging assignments, most notably the exchange officer position with the British army and as Commander/Director of the Foreign Science and Technology Center. My army-sponsored advanced schooling at Iowa State laid the foundation well for all these future assignments. I knew the Pentagon very well after two tours on the army staff and my final assignment on the staff of the Joint Chiefs of Staff. My wife and two daughters experienced all the hardships of my career with style and grace. We kept our strong family bond together through all the absences, changes and moves, and Sue made a home for us wherever we went. Their love and support sustained me throughout my army career.

BOND NEVER BROKEN

My lifetime friendship with Bob Ray and the circumstances that led us to be sitting next to each other on that airplane on that day, both surviving the crash, have been a major part of the narrative of my "airplane crash story" as it has evolved in my mind over the years. Bob Ray played perhaps the most significant role in the development of my feelings and thoughts on the airplane crash. He augmented my memories through our continued contact. For example, we called each other every year on 4 October to remind ourselves how fortunate we were to be alive and to renew our bond of friendship.

A year or so after the crash, Bob supplied me with a set of photographs of the crash site taken the day after the crash, and a copy of the June 1967 *Aviation Digest* in which a story of the airplane crash was featured. I began an "airplane crash" file and added to it whenever I gained any new information. At some point, Bob sent me a newspaper account of the tragic fate of the husband-and-wife medical team who were at the base camp hospital at An Khe and had the heated confrontation with Bob by his hospital bed. Whatever bits and pieces Bob sent me or I could collect, I added to the file.

My close contact with Bob Ray not only supplied me with more information about the crash but it allowed our families to get to know each other better. In 1974, when I was given a temporary "snowbird" assignment at the Army Personnel Center in Alexandria, Virginia, Bob and I reunited for a third time. Bob was assigned at the same location as the Chief of the Colonel's Branch of the Artillery. We both owned homes in Annandale, Virginia, and discovered that we were practically neighbors. That's when we decided to carpool to work each day, and we began a close family relationship with shared dinners and frequent visits.

On one such visit, I got an "order" from Bob and Peggy when I made my second trip to Iran in 1974 for a Persian rug (just something with blue in it). I remember well the happy scene after I returned and delivered the rug to their house. They seemed very pleased by my choice of color and design.

Of course, we swapped family stories and the progress of our kids as they went through school and various stages of life. Bob's son, Bobby, graduated from Princeton and became a well-known lawyer on the national scene.[7] We were also invited to the wedding of Bob and Peggy's daughter, Roseann, at the Army-Navy Country Club in Arlington where Bob maintained a membership for many years.

Bob and I remained in close contact, despite each of us going on to other assignments in the Washington, DC, area. I retired from the army in 1984, and Bob retired from the army in 1986. Bob and Peggy maintained their home in the Sleepy Hollow section of Annandale after we moved to Syracuse (1984–90) and then to Medford, New Jersey (1990 to present).

Around 2000, we became aware of Bob's Parkinson disease, and the remainder of our association was marked by watching this debilitating disease take a hold on Bob. Both our daughters were living in Virginia at that time, and when we visited them, we did not miss a chance to also visit Bob and Peggy.

During each visit, we saw the awful progress of this disease. Bob and Peggy displayed exceptional optimism, courage, and faith throughout, and our visits were always joyful and reaffirming of our friendship and special bond. At one point, I took Communion to Bob from St. Mary of the Lakes church in Medford and gave it to him in a very emotional moment when we arrived. Peggy, tiny as she was, would act as a walker for Bob, walking backwards with her hands on Bob's shoulders to hold and guide him from place to place during our visits. We had maintained contact by letters, phone, and email all the years since our ill-fated reunion on the Caribou. For example, in 2009, Bob and Peggy wrote to recommend a book which included accounts of events that had taken place in Vietnam during our time there. I responded to Bob and Peggy as follows:

14 May 2009

Dear Bob and Peggy,

I went through Amazon and bought a copy of Outrageous Hero per your enthusiastic recommendation. You were right on—it was a fantastic read. B.T. Collins must have been a remarkable human being, and you can easily recognize the love and esteem his sister had for him in writing the book.

Of course, for us, it was the chapters on Vietnam, 1st Cav Div, An Khe, et al, in 1966–67 that brings it all home. I have never been so proud of anything I've done in my life than volunteer for duty in Vietnam. It is so hard to recreate all the emotion and conflict taking place at that time (and afterwards), but B.T. Collins not only brought it back, but he placed it all in proper context of patriotism and concern for one another. I'm proud to place this book on my bookshelf of favorites. I hope to refer to it often.

I know the shadows are lengthening when at the West Point Founders Day Dinner this past March (held at the Union League in downtown Philly), I turned out to be the "oldest grad" signed up to attend. As such, I had the "honor and privilege" of giving the traditional "old grad" speech. To balance it, tradition has the "youngest grad" give a follow up speech. Both speeches turned out well. The superintendent and the new football coach were in attendance. I used a couple of stories as my crutch in getting through the speech—the first one on the light side and the other more serious. In the first story, I told of being "gigged" during an in-ranks inspection during my plebe year in 1953 by none other than (then) Major Alexander Haig. My egregious sin was having my cuff links on backwards! Honest-to-God true story! My second story told of my medevac through Clark AFB in 1966 and being given a bath by Kitsy Westmoreland. I must have hit the right chord—I got a very positive response. Of course, it amazed me to think I was talking of events that took place long before most of the audience (to include the superintendent) were even graduated from West Point. I dare say, some in the audience weren't even born yet! I was pleased to be able to relate something of that time that was so huge for us.

Sue and I are still hanging in there. The bishop of Trenton said I could "retire" from the diaconate at age 75, but he allowed me to keep my faculties (baptism, marriage, preach, etc.) as long as I am able. We stay busy with the garden and the grandchildren. We have a graduation every year for the next five years which brings great joy and satisfaction. Oldest grandson assigned to the carrier Ronald Reagan and is ready to depart for his second six-month deployment. We are very proud of him and the service he is giving.

Thanks for pointing the marvelous and inspiring book of B.T. Collins our way. We send our love and regards and truly wish there were a way we could be closer to share our memories and friendship.

Sincerely,
Joe and Sue

MILLION MILE CLUB

"I began a second career for 14 years with General Electric/ Martin Marietta/Lockheed Martin—same job, different bosses, as Program Manager for the Counter Battery Radar (COBRA). I lived this program from its concept, sold it as a package to the governments of France, Germany, and United Kingdom, and retired in 1999 after the first three prototypes were built. A very satisfying experience."

After retiring from the army in 1984, I began a second career with the defense industry. I worked initially for General Electric in Syracuse on a counter battery radar employing state-of-the-art technology. We sold our house in Annandale and moved to Syracuse, New York, for the next five years. The program involved working with radar firms in the United Kingdom, France, and Germany with the intent of selling the developed radar to the armed forces of these nations. This required extensive overseas travel to Europe and later to the Middle East. I qualified for the Million Mile Club initially with Pan Am and later with Delta Airlines.

When General Electric bought RCA in 1990, a major shift of programs took place, and I was caught up in the movement of my radar program to Moorestown, New Jersey. We sold our house in Syracuse and moved for the last time to Medford, New Jersey, the twenty-sixth move in our married life.

LIFE CHANGES

"My latest venture occurred when I entered the diaconate program in the Diocese of Trenton just prior to my second retirement and I was ordained a deacon in 2002."

Mark Twain challenged the world with the question: "What are the two most important days in your life?" The wisdom of the answer he gave has stayed with me all my life:

> *The first is the day you are born.*
> *The second is the day you find out why.*

We all search for the "why" answer, and in my case, I realize that my search evolved as part of a continual conversion process. How tempting it would be to say that my "why" answer was given to me after surviving the plane crash. It certainly shaped my outlook and pointed me in that direction, but my answer finally came when I made the decision to become an ordained deacon in the Catholic Church.

In 1998, thirty-two years after the plane crash, I began the four-year formation process to become a deacon. I have had numerous "stuck" points in my life, both before and after the plane crash, where things had to be resolved and some sort of transformation had to take place in my life. With humility and gratitude, I have been able to resolve most of these challenges throughout my life, and the transportive results have always been positive and beneficial for me.

I consider the plane crash, even now, as one of those transforming stuck points. I sincerely believe that at the end of each challenge in my life, resolution and transformation came about through my prayers and faith in God. No, I did not suddenly find this faith in God just after surviving the crash, although that would have been reason enough. This faith in God is part of a spiritual journey that I started early in life and has continued throughout my life and will likely not end until I enter the final mystery of death.

RETIREMENT

"It's been 26 moves since I walked through that sally port, but life seems to have settled down now around Medford, NJ, St. Mary of the Lakes Parish, our condo in Brigantine, our daughters and their great husbands, and our five wonderful grandchildren."

In 1999, another major life change occurred when I retired from Lockheed Martin. My "retirement" was followed by eighteen gratifying and fulfilling years serving as a deacon in the St. Mary of the Lakes Parish in Medford, New Jersey, until I retired from this clerical role in 2020.

Retirement has been joyfully spent in doing retired husband duties, being "spoiled" by my two daughters living close by and being a grandfather to five wonderful grandchildren. And now I'm a great-grandfather to five even more wonderous great granddaughters! I take great contentment in doing ancestry research, gardening, reading, sailing (member of the Brigantine Yacht Club and past commodore), and serving as secretary of the Sandpiper Condominium Association board of governors. Unfortunately, my contentment was shattered by the wild idea that I might even write a book!

Deacon Joe Retirement

Dear SML Parishioners,

I will be retiring from active diaconate ministry (for real this time!) The extended lock down has provided the opportunity for my wife Sue and I to reflect on this decision. As a couple of aging seniors, we recognize our limitations and see the need to pay more attention to our health issues. Fr. Dan, has been most sympathetic and understanding in approving our decision.

With truly great reluctance do we step away from diaconate ministry at St. Mary of the Lakes. Sue and I plan to continue living in Medford and to remain active members of SML parish. The 18 years serving as a deacon at SML have been the most rewarding and satisfying among the many phases of our lives. It has been an honor and a privilege to serve the wonderful priests and parishioners of the SML parish. The people of SML will always hold a special place in our hearts. Thank you!

Deacon Joe and Sue Tedeschi

Joe's retirement from the deaconate announced
St. Mary of the Lakes Parish Bulletin, June 21, 2020 (Medford, NJ)

CHAPTER 21
FIRST SURVIVOR CONTACT

I HAD LIVED WITH the memories of the crash every day since 4 October 1966, but I never attempted to commit these memories to paper. Then in 1987, I received a letter from a fellow survivor, Jordan Brindley, asking for my help in substantiating a disability claim he was making with the Veterans Administration for injuries he had received in the crash. Our exchanges were my first attempt to document the crash from my perspective.

January 22, 1987

Col. Tedeschi,

    Sir, I just spoke with your friend Rob Ray last evening on the phone. Our conversation was about the crash of the Caribou aircraft on the Hon Cong Mountain in An Khe on October 4, 1966. I was also one of the survivors of that crash and I was so glad to speak with Rob about it.

    My reasons for trying to locate other survivors is a problem I'm having with the VA. I suffered a lot of damage from my seatbelt as well as many other injuries. I remembered Major Ray because he, like yourself and I, were [sic] near the very tail end of the aircraft. Also Don Madden, remember the guy with the M-16 through his lower abdomen?

I belong to the 1st Cavalry's Division Association, and that's where I came up with Rob's address.

Rob agreed to help me all he could; he has offered to make copies of what records he still has. What I need is supporting statements from anyone who was involved as my medical records were apparently lost in the process of my air-evac from Vietnam to Jamma Army Hospital in Japan. I have only been able to get service connection [disability] on hearing loss and a fracture of my collarbone, but they (the VA) don't even want to talk to me about the other things, muscle damage, nerve damage, just to mention a few.

I would greatly appreciate any information or statement you could give; it would help my case greatly.

I'll include my P.N. and address on the next page and, again, thanks for any help you may offer. Even if you have no records or info, please, as a fellow survivor, let me wish you the very best.

Thank you again, sir,
Jordan Brindley, Jr.
Austin, TX

January 28, 1987

Mr. Jordan Brindley, Jr.
Austin, TX

Dear Jordan,

Your letter came as quite a surprise to me—not that I had forgot about the plane crash (who ever could!) but that I had [not] heard from another survivor other than Bob Ray. Bob Ray and I have seen quite a bit of each other since the plane crash—we were practically neighbors in Virginia. We even knew each other for some years prior to the crash, which makes it quite a coincidence that we were sitting next to each other when it happened.

I would be delighted to help out in any way that I can. Even though over twenty years have passed since the crash, I can remember quite a few details. I was one of the few people who was still conscious immediately following the crash—I don't remember blacking out at all. I have my medical records which document the fact that I was in the crash and that I suffered a dislocated and broken hip. These were essential when I retired in 1984 and was evaluated by the VA for disability. If these would be helpful to you, I would be glad to make copies and send them to you. I am enclosing a magazine article from the June 1967 US Army Aviation Digest which describes the crash and the causes of the crash. Perhaps this might be of some use to you.

Other than the above, I would need to know more precisely what you need in the way of documentation. It would seem that you have to establish that you were in the plane at the time of the crash—perhaps this is already established. I could then try to describe what I remember—the various people around me and the injuries as best as I can remember them. Bob Ray's injuries are easy for me to remember. The seat belt had torn into his stomach, and he was hemorrhaging internally. His face was white as a sheet. I remember vividly the man (you identified him as Don Madden) with the M-16 through his stomach. He kept calling out to me for help, but there was nothing I could do because I could not move due to my broken hip. I also remember the wounded man we had on board who had been in the stretcher and who ended up with even more injuries as a result of the crash. Perhaps you were the one next to me to whom I gave my .45 caliber pistol, and we tried to open the door to fire distress shots in groups of three. If so, you will remember the difficult time we had in trying to open the door because we did not realize the airplane was upside down, and we were all lying on the roof of the plane, and the door handle had to be turned in the opposite direction!

Please let me know what you need. I would gladly make a statement concerning the injuries I witnessed, the severity of the plane crash, the condition of the airplane following the crash (I have a set of photographs which Bob Ray gave me some time after the crash which show the crash site and the wrecked airplane) and the effect the seat belts may have had on causing injuries. I also vividly recall what a "clean" airplane it was following the crash, i.e., the fact that all the bucket seats and seat belts had given way at the impact, and we all ended up in a football pile of people, bucket seats, seatbelts wrapped around us, etc.—all in the middle of the airplane.

I certainly hope to hear from you again with a request for more help if you need it. In the meantime, my best regards to you, and I sincerely hope the years have treated you well since that eventful day on 4 October 1966. We share quite an experience—one that not many people can live to tell about. I have had to do a considerable amount of flying since that time, but I will never be comfortable flying ever again. My job takes me overseas quite often, and whenever we fly through fog, I become extremely nervous and uncomfortable. I have to bear it by myself—it is difficult to tell the people around you how you feel and why. I often wonder if they would believe me if I told them!

Sincere regards,
Joe Tedeschi

February 3, 1987

Mr. Joe Tedeschi
Fayetteville, NY 13066

Dear Joe,

I received your letter two days ago, and was it grand hearing from you, and I'm thankful for you and am glad you're doing well. I am proud for you and your family. I too am very happy with all the good that has come our way (myself and my family) since that day you and I and the others shared almost twenty years ago. And yes, I share your many feelings and mistrust in aircraft even today.

Yes Joe, I remember trying to get the darn door open on the Caribou, and it seemed to take forever before anyone got to us, let alone getting us up the side of Hon Cong Mountain.

From An Khe I went on to Qui Non and then to Jamma Army Hospital in Japan. [Jamma was the GI slang term for Yokahama. Likely the same one I was in, the 106th General Hospital.] I'm sorry, but I don't remember names but more the pain and suffering we all went through.

I do remember Rob and as you had said how drained he looked. I was a little more fortunate, my knees were banged up pretty good (from falling and landing on them) from the top (actually the bottom) of the aircraft. Most of my injuries were due to the seat belt; the chest muscles and nerves were totally severed on my left upper chest to about a quarter around my back on the left side. Perhaps you can recall me since you were conscious during the crash. I hung almost upside down for a few moments after we made the second impact then fell into the pile of people in the plane. I was a young "buck" sergeant and was returning from Dog LZ [landing zone] I think to get supplies for my company, the 1/12th Infantry. My C.O. was Captain Don F. Warren, I was his R.T.O. prior to that. You may remember my company because not too long before that we had our entire weapons platoon wiped out on another operation. Tom Castion of Look Magazine was with them at the time.

I can't locate Don Warren, but I did find my battalion C.O., Col. James T. Root. He remembered the crash and a lot of the operations we were on but didn't know where Capt. Warren was now.

I belong to the 1st Cav. Association and only live about an hour drive from Ft. Hood. I went up there some time back, and the P.O. officer took me on a grand tour. I met the Division C.O. and three or four of the division's chaplains; one of them knew Chap. Lord; he was on top of Hon Cong when they got us to the top.

. . . It seems I could go on forever, but yourself and Rob Ray will just have to get to one of the division's reunions. I would like to see you both. Anyone who shared Vietnam has something no one else has in common.

I sent for all the crash info from the Army Safety Center in Ft. Rucker, AL. I spoke with a Maj. Getappie, and he said the info he was sending me was pretty complete: names, injuries, survivors, and general info about the crash. As soon as I get it, I'll make copies and send to you and Rob. I know he hasn't settled with the VA yet, so it may be of help to him.

My problem is some of my records must have been lost as the VA says they have no record of seat belt injuries to my chest nor damage to my knees. I've written the medical records center in St. Louis, but if they had them, looks like the VA would also. I was young (twenty-one) and didn't have a lot of problems before, but now I'm forty-two, and I feel like I'm coming apart at the seams.

Any statement has to be notarized, so says the VA.

Yes, I do think it might help me if you did prepare a statement about the crash and anything you remember, even if you can't recall me by name of what I've told you. Rob said you had been in the hospital in Japan. Was it Jamma? My doctor was a Capt. Lee.

I filed my first claim in 1967 after I ETSed [expiration – term of service], but then as now, VA said they had no records, so I was not [given] service connected [benefits/disability]. I should have pursued it then, but in all truth, I was glad to be alive and be home. Seems hindsight always catches up with ya.

The paperwork from Ft. Rucker will confirm I was on the aircraft, but I'm not sure how in depth the medical data will be. I even have a statement from my civilian doctors stating the muscle and nerve damage, but that's all to be presented to the VA next month.

My VA service officer (not connected to the VA) is a super guy, but he too says we have a ways to go, that I need a witness...

Rob is going to call me when he gets back, so I'll let him know by phone what the stuff from Ft. Rucker looks like, but in the meantime, anything you can do, I'll be in your debt.

My warmest regards to your family.

Sincere regards,
J. Brindley, Jr.

P.S. I am sure of one thing, we all had seat belt injuries, and yes, I would like copies of the photos you have.

February 21, 1987

Mr. Jordan Brindley, Jr.
Austin, TX

Dear Jordan,

I received your second letter and have been trying to respond to it since then. It took me a little time to get the set of photographs recopied. I enclose this set and a notarized statement about what I can recall of the crash. Please note the dates—I am finishing this letter on 21 February but cannot get it notarized until I return from a trip to Munich next week. More flying—ouch! We have a notary public at work, but I will not be able to get to him until I return from the Munich trip.

Once again, please let me know if this is the kind of thing you are looking for. I really wish you good luck with the VA. They were very decent to me, and it sounds as if they are trying to do the same for you. It really is a shame that you did not pursue the matter back in '67 when things were fresher in people's minds and the records might have still been traceable. By the time I retired from the Army, all my X-rays from the first ones they took right after the crash to those after the operations and several taken years later at various physical exams were all lost. Fortunately, all one has to do is take an X-ray of my right hip, and the evidence is all still there. I still carry two good-sized screws (Phillips head) in my right hip which are holding my acetabulum (hip socket) together.

Again, I hope to continue to hear from you, especially if you are in the need of more supportive material. Perhaps there might be a time out there in the future when a "crash" reunion might be organized. Let's hope so. It would be a fantastic experience to see the survivors of that crash again. In the meantime, best regards to you and your family.

Sincerely,
Joe Tedeschi

Attachment: Affidavit of Crash

I would have to say from reading the letters again that Jordan was the soldier in my narrative that evolved from the pile of people to open the door of the upside-down airplane. After my last letter to Jordan, I did not hear from him again to find out the progress of his VA claim. But I did track him down another twenty-two years later to find he was still around and willing to review my manuscript!

AFFIDAVIT OF CRASH

19 February 1987
Fayetteville, NY

To Whom It May Concern:

On 4 October 1966, I was in an airplane crash in Vietnam. I was a passenger in a C-7 Caribou military aircraft returning to the 1st Air Cav Base Camp at An Khe. The weather was foggy, and at the time of the crash, the aircraft was flying through completely foggy conditions. The aircraft was attempting to land at the base camp airfield under GCA conditions. The wheels were down, and it seemed that we were in our approach path when the crash occurred. At the time of the crash, it was difficult to understand what was happening. There were two impacts. The first impact was the right wing hitting a tree. This impact tore off the right wing, and the airplane flipped over. The second impact followed almost immediately the first. This was the airplane plowing into the side of the mountain. I later found out that the pilot had misjudged his altitude and bearing on his approach to the airfield. There were problems with the GCA radar, and the pilot thought he was lined up with the airfield but was about a mile off. As a result, he flew the airplane into Hong Kong [sic] Mountain which dominated the terrain around the An Khe base camp.

There were 31 personnel aboard the aircraft. From reports that I heard later, about half these people were killed in the crash. I was sitting in the second to last seat on the port side of the aircraft. In the last seat next to me was then-LTC Bob Ray. I did not know any of the other passengers before the crash. I was conscious throughout the crash and the time until rescuers arrived.

Following the second impact, I can remember being tossed about and ending up on the back end of what I can only describe as a football pile of people, seats (these were bucket seats—a row along each side of the aircraft), and being wrapped in my seat belt. We had all been buckled up in seat belts at the time of the crash, but the force of the impact was such that the bucket seats and the seat belts all gave way, and it was a completely "clean" airplane from the rear to the pile of people which had been thrown to the middle of the aircraft. I suffered a dislocated and fractured hip as a result of the crash. My injuries were such that I could only crawl a few feet. There were a number of injured and dead people about me. I recall several other survivors being conscious, and we attempted to do whatever we could to alleviate the situation. At the time, we did not realize that we were lying on the roof of the aircraft because the airplane had flipped over after the first impact. We attempted to open the side door but had great difficulty because we did not realize the airplane was upside down, and the door handle turned in the opposite direction. I gave my pistol to the man nearest the door, and he fired distress signal shots in volleys of three. Rescuers arrived on the scene in about 30 minutes. There was no explosion or fire as a result of the crash.

The survivors were sorted out by the severity of their injuries, and rescue attempts were made by bringing in helicopters to take out the injured. They tried first to use Hueys, but they were unsuccessful. They next tried the Chinooks, but the helicopters could not get low enough to use their rescue winches. Attempts were made to clear the tree branches with chain saws so the helicopters could fly in closer, but it became too dark by this time, and the decision was made to man-pack all the injured to the top of the mountain. From there, the injured were flown to the base camp hospital.

I can testify to the severity of the injuries suffered as a result of the crash. I am familiar with LTC Ray's injuries because he was next to me during the crash. The seat belt had cut into his abdomen and caused internal hemorrhaging. My hip was fractured and dislocated, possibly as a result of the strain of the seat belt along the side of my body. The force of the impact of the crash was enough to drive an M-16 rifle through the stomach of one of the men on board.

In the case of Jordan Brindley, although I do not remember him specifically, I can readily believe that the seat belt could have caused the nerve and muscle damage he describes. As I understand his injuries, the chest muscles and nerves were totally severed on his left upper chest to about a quarter around his back on the left side. This would describe exactly the points of stress the seat belt and shoulder harness would place upon the body during a violent crash of the severity we experienced. I know the seat belt caused LTC Ray's injuries and very possibly mine as well. In all fairness to the seat belt and harness, they probably saved our lives as well.

Joseph R. Tedeschi
Col. (Ret) US Army

SOMETHING IN WRITING

When I wrote the affidavit for Jordan, it was the first time I had written out a description of the crash from memory. This fixed in my mind some of the details I remembered of the crash, and I had a real sense of relief that I finally had something in writing. Our letter exchanges were important to my finally putting together the story and documenting it. This also provided the seed of my eventual book. I placed this affidavit in my "airplane crash file" I had been keeping and temporarily forgot it.

In 1998 and 1999, as I was going through my diaconate and retirement life transitions, I decided to expand on the affidavit in the form of a memoir. My inspiration to do so was prompted by a desire to leave something to my grandchildren as a vignette of my wartime experience in Vietnam. I titled the memoir "A Rock in the Clouds."

In 2007, I was offered the opportunity to submit a second submission in addition to my bio for the Class of 1957 Anniversary Yearbook. The organizers wanted to record in a section of the yearbook the wartime history of class members. The instructions for preparing the input were in part:

> It is a major section and a difficult section; its interest and importance will depend on the information you all provide us. We need information on your combat assignments/ experiences in any conflicts since graduation . . . Stories and photos involving you and other classmates . . . will add interest . . .

I had my brief combat assignment in Vietnam and the experience of the plane crash to offer. I remembered the memoir I had already written in 1998, and I initially was inclined to offer a slightly revised account along with photos of the crash to the yearbook organizers. But then I began to have second thoughts about doing so because I really did not feel it was worthy enough to be submitted. I wondered whether the memoir would stand up alongside the incredible record and actions of so many of my classmates in Vietnam. After all, surviving a plane crash would seem to be a matter of "luck of the draw," and the incident of the plane crash just a result of another wartime accident.

With this in mind, I asked a couple of close classmate friends whether I should submit my account of the crash to the class as wartime history. They read my memoir, and they both encouraged me to submit it. I eventually did so, but it was edited to fit the space requirements of the yearbook. Even so, I felt deeply honored that my classmates decided to accept it alongside the valorous accounts of so many other classmates, and especially the twelve hero classmates who died fighting in Vietnam.

Just having the abbreviated account of the plane crash included in the Class of 1957 Fiftieth Anniversary Yearbook inspired me, and I continued to toy with the idea of turning my memoir into a book. But I realized that I just did not have enough supporting material, so I placed the revised memoir in my "crash" file along with Jordan Brindley's correspondence and several other items I had collected about the crash over the years, and I allowed the idea to fester.

CHAPTER 22
A NEW WORLD OF DISCOVERY

I STILL HAD MANY unanswered questions and concerns about the crash in my mind. There were so many more details I wanted to know, but my resources for discovery were dwindling with time, and it seemed I would have to be content with the knowledge I already had. But in 2009, I became acquainted with the Vietnam Memorial Virtual Wall on the internet (http://www.virtualwall.org). With this, a whole new world of discovery and information about the plane crash suddenly and unexpectedly opened up to me. I wrote the following email to Bob and Peggy Ray and excitedly shared my discovery with them.

---

26 March 2010

Hi Bob and Peggy,

A friend sent me the website for the VN Virtual Wall which is http://www.virtualwall.org/iStates.htm. It is a remarkable site in which one can move around quite easily and pinpoint names, dates, etc. Each individual has a designated page with detailed information of the death, time, place, etc., with even places for memorial tributes from family and friends. [It's unfortunate this feature has not been available to update for some time.]

Naturally curious, I started out by clicking on "Find a Name" which gives a drop-down menu. From the drop-down menu, I selected "Wall Panels by Date." This gives you a page listing all the wall panels. Select Wall Panel 11E with dates from 9/22/1966 to 10/31/1966. This gives a picture of the Wall Panel 11E with all the names on it. Drop down to the line beginning with the name "Philip M. Callan." To the right of this name is the first name of those killed in the plane crash on 4 Oct 1966—Henry Lee Creek. [Later I found names were listed by the date of death and then in alphabetical order, and the names began on the line above.] The info I'm enclosing on Henry Lee Creek is located within the pages that follow when you click on his name. You can do the same for all the others (totaling 13) who were killed in the crash.

The information on the matching up of the Army and Air Force aviation units at the time they were transferring responsibility for the C-7 is interesting. Our crew was 3 AF and 1 Army (SP4 Bird). Interesting, too, is the way the AF designated the crash due to hostile action, while the Army did not. The 3 AF members received the Purple Heart as a result. We clearly know it was not due to hostile action, but it does seem uneven and not balanced that one service should look at it one way, and the other service just the opposite. Really "small potatoes" at this point, but interesting from an historical point of view.

Pray all is going well with you both. You are in our thoughts and prayers.

Sincerely,

Joe

THE VIRTUAL WALL ® VIETNAM VETERANS MEMORIAL   www.VIRTUALWALL.org

Find A Name ▼	The Virtual Wall ® ▼

Panel 11E of the Vietnam Veterans Memorial

Casualty dates 9/22/1966 through 10/31/1966.

<< Panel 10 E - Earlier   **Later - Panel 12 E >>**

Point to any name for the line number and casualty date of the first name on the line.
Click on any name to see that person's memorial page on The Virtual Wall. ®

WALTER L WELLS JOHN D WILLIAMS GEORGE WYCINSKY Jr RAYMOND E FLEMING Jr GERALD W BRASCHE
EMANUEL F DRUMMOND Jr DAVID R AIKEN ROBERT W GARTH Jr LLOYD L GOODING SALVATORE GUARINO
PAUL G HAZEN RAY W HOLEMAN FRANK C HUBICSAK JIMMY A JOHNSON NOE MAGALLAN
ANTONIO R OSUNA WILLIAM P PRESSON Jr LARRY LEE REYNOLDS DAVID R WARGO WILLIAM M SHETRON
OLIN R THRUSH CARMELO ROMAN-AGUILAR JOSEPH T WILLIAMS JOHN T KLUMP ELMER L BUCHANAN
STEPHEN E BURTON ALFREDO CASTANON ESTILL L CHILDERS JACK E CROUCH Jr GARRY D DAVIS
CECIL E DORSEY WILLIAM E EBEL WAYNE E ELLISON JOHN H FULCHER JAMES E GRAHAM Jr WAYNE E BENGE
ROBERT C HAUSER GERALD J BANNACH BURNS W KNOWLTON Jr REXFORD A LAROCK EDWIN J LUCKSTEAD
JOHN C LYNCH JEAN USZAKOW ROBERT P MINOR HOWARD G MORRISON GERALD C Mc KEEN
VERNON L RAMEY WILBURN ROBERSON DAVID J ROSE DANIEL J RUSNELL ROBERT P SANTOR
DWIGHT K SATTERWHITE LARRY GENE SHEFFIELD WAYNE T STRICKLAND CLYDE MINIX JUNIOR L WHITTLE
STEPHEN A ANDERSON GARY A BARNARD JOHN J BARZAN WILLIAM R BEASLEY PETER R BOSSMAN
LARRY J CALLOWAY RONALD M CRAWN CLIFTON E CUSHMAN GARY R DOPP PHILLIP A DUCAT
ROBERT D FELLOWS CHARLES L FORD HERMON E FULLER Jr ARTHUR W GREEN DONALD M HENRICKS Jr
JAMES E HOLDER ROY D HUTTING HOWARD W JACKSON BRUCE L KENNEDY ERNEST R MARTIE
JAMES E MILLER JERRY L NEWBRAND RONNIE LEE NOSEFF VERNON H PARKER Jr JERRY D PILLSBURY
DAVID W POLICH TERRY L PUNDSACK LOUIS R RANDALL DEAN W REITER KARL A SCHMIDT Jr
JAMES D STALLINGS PAUL D TICE JEFFREY P VAUGHN ROBERT M WATERS LARRY W WHITCOME
LAWRENCE WILLIAMS Jr WALTER WILLIAMS Jr REGINALD L CONE NORMAN L DUPRE ROBERT F GRUNDMAN
JAMES W HOLLIDAY RICHARD C JOHNSON HENRY L MOSBURG GARY R PARSONS MARVIN F PHILLIPS
JERRY W ROSS CHARLES W TURNER CHARLES M CENTENO FRANK E DZIWISZ Jr ARVEL H HALL
RONALD G JORDET LAWRENCE F KINNEAR BILLY W LAWS THOMAS A LOWDEN WILLIAM R MASTERS
GROVER C MATHEWS Jr GARY P MEYER CARROLL W POWELL ROBERT E ROBINSON JAMES W ROWLETT
DYKE A SPILMAN VICKEY E STANLEY JOSEPH M STINE GARRETT G SUTTON Jr ISTVAN SZABO
CHARLES S BURNS III JOHN W GEARY JAMES R HANSON DENNIS T HAYWORTH DANIEL C JONES
KENNETH A KEITH JULIO I MARTIR-TORRES GEORGE G MOLINA MIGUEL F NAJAR GEORGE E O'NEILL
THOMAS J ONTIVEROS GREGG E REED RANDELL F SHANNON LONNIE D SPROUSE DANNY G TAYLOR
RALPH G TILL BENNY E WIMBERLY JACKIE RAY BROWN JACK CAMPBELL JAMES M HARGROVE
WALTER MARCUM CRISTOBAL MELENDEZ BOOKER SMITH Jr SAUL WAXMAN THOMAS L WESTPOINT
LANHAM O BROYLES ELMER E COTNEY WILLIAM T DEUEL LOUIS P GAGNE Jr IRVIN J HOPKINS
JOHN T LOGAN RICHARD T MALASPINA HENRY O MARTIN III DAVID I MUSCH RICHARD A SMITH
TERRY LEE SNYDER ROGER L BONNER Jr RICHARD L BISHOP MICHAEL J DE MARSICO CURTIS L FITZPATRICK Jr
LEROY FRAZIER WENDELL R GRIZZLE JOE C KELLEY JOE H MOOREHEAD TRAVIS E NUNNERY
WILLIAM L STUBBE EDWARD A URIBE RODRICK P WHALEN JOHN D ANDRADE LARRY W BAILEY
THOMAS E BEGLINGER BOBBY RAY BRYANT RICHARD F WALTERS PEPITO CAGUIMBAL JIMMIE DELL GRAY
LOUIS E HADDOCK Jr TERRY E HEMMITT VICTOR E KUHNS DOUGLAS R LUECK RONALD H MIS
WALTER A MURZIN DUNCAN A MacFETTERS FLORENTINO R ROQUE FRANCIS P ROYAL ROY SALAZAR
BELMIRO TAVARES Jr DALE A WAID MICHAEL L BYAM KENNETH O ALFSTAD BILLY J CLAYTON
JAMES A DANIELS RAYMOND L ECHEVARRIA RANDAL C ENGRAM JAMES H GRAFF WILLIE GREEN Jr
JOHN M HENS EDDIE LEE WILLIAMS GEORGE A WALDRON JOHNNIE LEE LAWRENCE KENNETH A MALLONEE
JOHN W MARTIN GREGORY D Mc KEAGUE RICHARD A ROSBECK JEROME J SMITH DAVID A THORPE
HOWARD D ULMER Jr JAMES E JONES BENJAMIN I WARREN RAYMOND L WHEELER DENNIS L WILLIAMS
HAROLD H HIRTLE GEORGE W ALEXANDER Jr JOHN T BIRD FRANCIS H BISSAILLON CHARLES M BRADFORD
PHILIP M CALLAN HENRY L CREEK SAM W DAILY JOHNNIE L DANIEL JOHN P EYNON THOMAS H TREBATOSKI
JOHN H JONES RONALD E LEWIS JAMES G LITTS PINK M LYNCH Jr DANIEL P MARLOWE ROBERT O KORNS
PHILLIP MILLER RAYFORD J MOSLEY HOMER L PICKETT RICHARD M PROCIV ARMANDO RAMOS
AUGUSTINE D RUSSO DONALD A SMITH Jr RONALD K STANEART ROBERT J STEEL DAVID O WEBSTER
KENNETH W WEST WILLIAM R ANDREWS JAMES A BEENE DAVID J BOHN JAMES J CARROLL
ROBERT G DAVIDSON JOHN G DICKERSON III ALBERT E HUFFER MERLIN P LEGAUX PAUL H MITCHELL Jr
DAVID L OWENS JOSH PALM Jr WALTER F PAYNE JOHN R SMITH RODNEY G THORNTON
JULIO C VARGAS ALBERT L VICICH MELVIN L STONE Jr GARY H BRUX THOMAS DEAN JOSEPH S HENRIQUEZ
ULYSSES V FRAZIER RICHARD M HECK ROBERT H HOLMES RICHARD E RICHARDSON ALFRED J KIBLER
RONALD W LEE JOSEPH A MOEN DAVID L MOSER RONALD E PFEIFER WILLIAM E JOHNSON

My first glimpse of the panel listing those lost in the crash

Henry Lee Creek
Private First Class
HHC, 1ST BN, 12TH CAVALRY, 1ST CAV DIV, USARV
Army of the United States
Dallas, Texas
December 04, 1943 to October 04, 1966
HENRY L CREEK is on the Wall at Panel 11E, Line 44
See the full profile or name rubbing for Henry Creek

The first name I identified from the panel [Henry Creek]

A Note from The Virtual Wall

The C-7 "Caribou" light transport was an Army aircraft, but early in the war a decision was taken to transfer them to the Air Force. The Army's six Caribou companies were matched up with an equal number of temporary Air Force squadrons, and the two groups worked together until the Air Force flight and maintenance crews were ready to stand on their own. The Army's 17th Aviation Company was paired with the Air Force's 6252nd Operations Squadron.

On 04 October 1966 C-7B *CARIBOU* tail number 63-9751 crashed into Hon Cong Mountain near An Khe Air Base, Binh Dinh Province. Thirteen men died in the crash:

- Flight crew:
  - Capt Francis H. Bissaillon, Williamstown, MA, 6252 Opns Sqdn, 7th AF
  - Capt David O. Webster, Phoenix, AZ, 6252 Opns Sqdn, 7th AF
  - SSgt Daniel P. Marlowe, San Antonio, TX, 6252 Opns Sqdn, 7th AF
  - SP4 John T. Bird, Summit, NJ, 17th Avn Co, 1 Cav Div

- Passengers:
  - CPT Johnnie L. Daniel, Johnston, SC, HHC, 1st Bde, 1 Cav Div
  - 1LT Kenneth W. West, Jacksonville, FL, B Btry, 2nd Bn, 19th Artillery
  - SFC Armando Ramos, Santurce, PR, A Co, 13th Sig Bn, 1 Cav Div
  - SSG Richard M. Prociv, Salt Lake City, UT, HHC, 1st Bde, 1 Cav Div
  - SGT Homer L. Pickett, Oklahoma City, OK, B Btry, 1st Bn, 21st Artillery
  - PFC James G. Litts, Bushkill, PA, HHC, 8th Eng Bn
  - PFC Henry L. Creek, Dallas, TX, HHC, 1st Bn, 12th Cavalry
  - PFC Ronald E. Lewis, Chicago, IL, B Co, 1st Bn, 5th Cavalry
  - PFC Donald A. Smith, Royal Oak, MI, A Co, 5th Bn, 7th Cavalry

Oddly, the three Air Force personnel are coded as hostile deaths, while the Army personnel are coded as non-hostile. There is no known evidence that the crash was due to hostile fire.

My first glimpse of a list of names of those who died that day

FURTHER SHARING MY DISCOVERY

On the occasion of Memorial Day in May of 2010, I was asked to give a reflection and a prayer for the opening party at the Brigantine Yacht Club. I was inspired by my recent discovery of The Virtual Wall, and so I used my new knowledge of the crash to encourage the attendees to make the gravity of the day more approachable:

I wonder if some of you share the problem I have when I ponder the almost countless numbers who made the ultimate sacrifice. My feelings and memories for this day tend to be diluted in the vastness of it all. And so, I would ask you to help me frame my prayer by focusing on at least one of the fallen, and by extension, we can include every last one of them.

I then led the gathering on the journey I had taken through the Vietnam Virtual Wall along with the circumstance of my survival of the crash. Its memorial pages had allowed me to come to a better understanding of what happened. I then encouraged the listeners,

My thought is this: if we can focus on these thirteen men, the meaning and purpose of Memorial Day might not be lost in the vastness of numbers. And if thirteen is still too much, let's focus on at least one of them. PFC Henry Lee Clark, HHC, 1st Battalion, 12th Cavalry, 1st Cavalry Division, Army of the United States. He was born in Dallas, Texas, on 4 December 1943, and just shy of his twenty-third birthday, he died in that airplane crash on 4 October 1966 . . .

And so, I would ask you frame your own prayer, to remember each in his own way, PFC Henry Lee Clark and the other twelve men who died in that airplane crash forty-four years ago, and then to extend your thoughts and prayers to every one of the countless brave men and women who died for our country in every war, especially now in Iraq and Afghanistan. Amen.

A DOMINO FALLS

This discovery of the Virtual Vietnam Wall was such a "breath of fresh air" for me after all these years of knowing almost nothing about the crash. For the first time in forty-five-plus years, I found the names (and photos in some cases), hometowns, and units of the those who died in the crash. I was also able to piece together the unit designations of the air force and army squadrons that were involved in the ongoing service transfer of the Caribou aircraft. The two units (6252 Operations Squadron, 7th AF and 17th Aviation Company, 1st Cavalry Division) were located next to each other at An Khe airfield (aka the "Golf Course"), and they flew joint missions (mixed crews) as part of the transfer process orientation.

After absorbing all this new information, I began to find other leads offered by this website using internet search engines. It seemed that one source of information led to another and then another, and by the beginning of 2020, through this fascinating and adventurous search of the internet, I had gathered more than sufficient new information and material about the crash, enough to fill a book. That's when I decided to gather all the new information and documents I had obtained and to revisit my original memoir. By this time, the idea of a book was "an itch I had to scratch." The lockdown period of the coronavirus pandemic gave me just the time I needed to begin writing.

My original game plan in writing the book was to take the "A Rock in the Clouds" memoir and expand it into a second part which I planned to title, *A Rock in the Clouds Revisited*. I took out my "plane crash" file and began to organize the original papers with all the supporting material I had gathered in the intervening years. Being a rank amateur at putting a book together, I soon came to realize that I needed some professional help in organizing all the material, and I sought and engaged an editorial service. This proved to be beneficial in many ways. In order to frame and more fully explain how the plane crash impacted my life, my editor suggested that I integrate parts of my life story both before and after the crash. In order to accomplish this, my original game plan for writing the book would have to be considerably expanded, and this book is the result.

CHAPTER 23
MAKING LIFE-CHANGING CONNECTIONS

DISCOVERING THE VIRTUAL WALL and its messages from friends and loved ones inspired me to do more searching for information, especially with the power of search engines on the internet. Starting with researching the aircraft that was involved in the crash, I found a page about the C-7A Caribou made by de Havilland of Canada.[8] The website gives a wealth of information and an excellent description of the C-7A.

It also allows visitors to the site to leave comments and questions. Taking a very long shot, I left a note on 4 October 2011 (same day as the crash but forty-five years later) in the "Comments" section (see second image next page).

De Havilland Canada DHC-4 Caribou

1958

TRANSPORT

Virtual Aircraft Museum / Canada / De Havilland Canada

The decision to build the de Havilland Canada DHC-4 Caribou was taken in 1956, the object being to develop an aircraft combining the load-carrying capability of the Douglas DC-3 with the STOL performance of the Beaver and Otter. The Canadian army placed an order for two and the US Army followed with five, the US Secretary of Defense waiving a restriction which limited the US Army to fixed-wing aircraft with an empty weight less than 2268kg.

The prototype flew in July 1958, its high wing having a characteristic centre-section with marked anhedral. The rear door was designed as a ramp for items weighing up to 3048kg. In the trooping role up to 32 soldiers could be carried. The Caribou served with the RCAF as the CC-108 and with the US Army as the AC-1 (1962 designation CV-2A). As a result of its evaluation of the first five aircraft the US Army adopted the Caribou as standard equipment and placed orders for 159.

The second batch of aircraft was designated CV-2B. Following tension on the border between China and India, the US Army handed over two Caribous to the Indian Air Force in early 1963. In January 1967 the 134 Caribous still in service with the US Army were transferred to US Air Force charge as C-7A and C-7B transports. The aircraft was a general sales success and examples flew not only with air forces throughout the world, but also with civil operators. In Canadian service the Caribou was replaced by the DHC-5 Buffalo and surplus examples were sold to a number of nations including Colombia, Oman and Tanzania. Many of the Canadian aircraft had been loaned to the United Nations, seeing extensive international service. Production ended in 1973. The DHC-4A model supplanted the DHC-4 on the production line from aircraft no. 24: the two models are very similar apart from the later model's increase in weight, maximum take-off weight of the DHC-4 being 11793kg. Total production was 307.

Aviastar Virtual Aircraft Museum De Havilland Caribou page

Comments 1-20 21-40 41-60

Joseph Tedeschi, e-mail, 10.04.2011 00:24

Was one of fortunate survivors of crash of C-7 into Hong Kong Mountain at An Khe on 4 Oct 1966. Thirteen were killed including air crew. Blinding fog and we flew right into mountain. Tree took off right wing and we augered in upside down. No explosion or fire. This tough airplane saved my life. I was med-evaced with broken hip, and never got to know full story and details of crash. Anyone have any info?

reply

Rodger Harrington, e-mail, 11.03.2011 17:16

I was lucky enough to have been crew chief on one of the caribous (AC-1) that comprised the 187th Trans Airplane Company,11th Air Assault at Ft. Benning tail number 62-4155.

Comment I posted on De Havilland Caribou page

FIRST CONTACT —TERRY HAMBY

Remarkably, a year and half later, I was elated to receive responses from two individuals who had seen this posting, both within weeks of each other. Terry Hamby of Coral Springs, Florida, emailed me first on February 17, 2013. He told me he "saw my post," and was himself a Caribou pilot in Vietnam in 1966.

I was so excited to hear from Terry and emailed him back that day:

Sent: Sun, Feb 17,2013
To: t . . . @comcast.net
From: Terry Hamby <b . . . @aol.com>
Subject: E-mail from Terry about the Caribou crash in Vietnam

Saw your post.

I was a baby-faced CW2 Army pilot in Vietnam in 1966. I flew with the 61st out of Vung Tau before we turned over the Caribous to the Air Force. The rumor about the crash in question was that the pilots had the ADF, which could also be used as the AM radio when tuned to an AM station, tuned to the local radio station and not to the ADF beacon used for the instrument approach in this case. So they homed in on the mountain and flew into it in the soup because the transmitting antenna for the radio station was on the mountain top.

I only shot one approach in weather during my year in country and that was a GCA into Saigon. It was zero/zero and because I had two miles of runway in front of me, I never broke it off at minimums (200 ft) which the protocol is if you can't see the runway by then, and we never saw the runway until the main gear touched dead on the centerline. Guess I just wanted bragging rights.

Terry Hamby
Coral Springs, FL
b . . . @aol.com

From: tedeschij <t . . . @comcast.net>
To: Terry Hamby <b . . . @aol.com>
Sent: Sun, Feb 17,2013 4:29 pm
Subject: Re: E-mail from Terry about the Caribou crash In Vietnam

Hi Terry,

What a great surprise to get your e-mail about the Caribou crash at An Khe. I have been trying for years to get more info on what happened. As one of the survivors, I have always wanted to get more info on the causes, the crew, and the other passengers. Once we got into medical evac channels, I lost contact with almost everyone else in the crash other than Col. Bob Ray who was sitting next to me on the airplane. He had his intestines cut by the seat belt but survived and served a full career afterwards. Regretfully, he is in a nursing home now in Alexandria, VA, with Parkinson's Disease—a result of Agent Orange exposure for sure. Not sure what you meant by "saw your post." Was that the note I left on the Virtual Wall web site? I also wrote a little account of the crash for my grandkids—was wondering if you saw that as well. If not, I would be happy to e-mail you a copy.

I would be very interested to know anything more you know about the crash. The info you gave me on the cause seems very plausible with the radio station on top of the mountain. I had a friend, Leo Keefe, involved with the Caribou Squadron at the time—name familiar?

My sincere thanks in responding after all these years. Obviously, this was a "turning point" in my life, and there isn't a day goes by without thinking of it and the guys involved. Hope to hear from you.

Joe Tedeschi

From: Terry Hamby <b . . .@aol.com>
To: t . . . @comcast.net
Sent: Sunday, February 17, 2013 6:39:10 PM
Subject: Re: E-mail from Terry about the Caribou crash in Vietnam

Joe,

 This was the post:
 >>>Joseph Tedeschi, t . . . @comcast.net 10.04.2011
 >>>Was one of fortunate survivors of crash of C-7 into Hong Kong
Mountain at An Khe on 4 Oct 1966 . . . Anyone have any info?<<<
 It was one of many comments located in the Virtual Aircraft Museum/
Canada/De Havilland site. It was under the "Caribou" page. I am going
to ask Bruce Silvey to forward this e-mail to the membership in the Army
Otter Caribou Association. I am sure there are several people that know
the real story on this crash, and they can fill us in or at least tell us where
to find the info online.

Terry

 Terry had referred to one of the Caribou pilot associations.[9] A
newsletter of the Air Force C7-A Caribou Association would turn out
to be another great source for additional information on the crash.

CHAPTER 24
OTHER WITNESSES ON THE SCENE

SECOND CONTACT – BOB BACH

A week after my exchanges with Hamby, I received an email from a second source, Bob Bach, who was stationed with an MP (military police) company at An Khe and one of the first responders on the crash scene.

From: "robert bach" <r . . . @gmail.com>
To: t . . . @comcast.net
Sent: Monday, February 25, 2013 10:03:36 AM
Subject: Oct. '66 Caribou Incident @ An Khe

Sir,

I found something on the web regarding an aircraft incident that occurred in October of 1966 at An Khe, South Vietnam. You indicated you were in a twin-engine Caribou that nosed into a 2300-foot tall mountain near the top. I was serving as an MP with the 504th Military Police in the town of An Khe and responded to that incident. My memory is sketchy (at best) but if I can provide any information for you, I will endeavor to do so.

From: tedeschij <t . . . @comcast.net>
To: "robert bach" <r . . . @gmail.com>
Sent: Mon, Feb 25, 2013 at 10:22 AM
Subject: Oct. '66 Caribou Incident @ An Khe

Hi Bob,

Great of you to answer my long-ago appeal for any info about the Caribou crash (I have info from the VN Virtual Wall website that has a short write-up about the crash which states that thirteen people were killed), but right after the crash, we were all med evaced away from the scene, so I only have bits and pieces about the other survivors, the crew, causes of the crash etc. I was sitting in the second to the last seat in the back of the airplane, and had my hip broken. Col. Bob Ray was sitting next to me in the last seat, and he survived as well with ruptured intestines (cut by his seatbelt). You may well have been one of the people who pulled me out of the airplane, and later man-packed us to the top of the mountain on stretchers (in the dark with flashlights as I recall). I also have memories of the rescuers trying to get us out with helicopters, but they just couldn't get them in close enough to hoist us out. Other than Bob Ray, I have not had any contact with other survivors or rescuers to get their stories. Bob is currently in a nursing home in Alexandria, VA, with Parkinson's disease as a result of exposure to Agent Orange I'm quite sure. We, of course, have shared our stories, and have kept contact all these years.

If you have any details of the crash, memories of the rescue, etc., I would be most grateful to get them from you. This event was obviously a "turning point" in my life, and not a day goes by that I don't think about it and all the other guys in the crash. Bob Ray was able to get a set of photos that were taken the next day of the crash scene which I have. If you like, I can e-mail them to you.

Again, many thanks for responding and remembering. Hard to believe it all took place forty-seven years ago!

From: "Robert Bach" <r . . . @gmail.com>
To: t . . . @comcast.net
Sent: Monday, February 25, 2013 12:48:05 PM
Subject: Re: Oct. '66 Caribou incident @ An Khe

Joe,

Nice to hear from you. I will be busy off-and-on this week but would like to talk to you . . .

I am retired, but I am heavily involved in emergency management and response.

If it is okay with you, let me have your phone number, and I will try to give you a call sometime soon.

My number is 5**-4**-9***

I was so anxious to get more information of the crash—especially from someone else who was actually on the scene—that I followed up on Bob's offer to talk on the phone and called him three days later on February 28, 2013. During the call to Bob Bach, I took handwritten notes during the phone conversation. Here I have recreated his account:

I remember the day of 4 October 1966 very well. It was overcast, muggy, and humid with a lot of water vapor in the air. I was with the 504th MP Company (Military Police) assigned to An Khe. I had been in the town of An Khe that day, and at the time of the crash, I happened to be back at base camp at the end of the airfield at An Khe.

I heard unusual aircraft noise that didn't sound right, and not much later, there was a crackle on the radio announcing an airplane crash. From the radio traffic, it soon became clear that something bad had happened. I decided to drive over to the checkpoint at the base of Hon Cong Mountain. This was about fifteen minutes after I heard the crash. I could not drive up the mountain in the jeep, so I started climbing.

It took me thirty-five to forty-five minutes to climb to the crash site because the mountain was heavily covered with vegetation. There were a number of other people also making their way toward the downed plane.

When I came up on the crash, a number of other people had already gathered. I could see the airplane buried into the side of the mountain with the tail of the airplane upside down and sticking in the air. Through the open door, the crush of people was visible inside.

They began to pull people out. Those who were dead, they covered with ponchos. One guy came out of the plane with an M-16 through him. They decided not to remove it from his groin at that point.

I walked over to a guy on the ground with a bad gash across his face, and just about the same time, up walked a guy who said he was a registered nurse from the base hospital who seemed to know what he was doing.

Helicopters were called in and hovered right over the crash site. I was one of the guys who strapped the guy with the gash on his face and leg injury into the wire stretcher to be hoisted up to the chopper. The Huey couldn't hold position with the stretcher dangling beneath it. The stretcher drifted back and forth like a pendulum and even dragged the guy on it through the trees.

They lowered the stretcher back down again with a bounce. The registered nurse, a 1st Lieutenant, felt that they had to get this injured soldier medevaced, so they tried again. The guy got his arm out of the stretcher to keep from banging into the trees. Swinging thirty or forty feet in the air, this guy thought he was going to be killed. Finally, they decided to call off the helicopters and carry the wounded to the top of the mountain. It was a really steep grade leading to the top.

A large number of people finally arrived at the site. I couldn't believe all of the ones only standing around taking pictures! [In a follow-up email, Bob says there were more doing that than trying to help with the injured.] A brigade commander arrived on scene. He called for electrical generators to be brought in. Since I had my MP hat on and a two-way radio, they used me as the communication link with the people at the top of the mountain. This allowed them to coordinate the rescue.

In about thirty minutes, the whole scene became very dark with the sun going down. People started popping flares to give light—you would hear this "woosh" of the parachutes as the flares were sent up. Once I made the radio call to bring in generators, the flares stopped, although the generators did not arrive until around midnight.

With the lights from the generators, they worked all night, and I was not released until the morning. [After evacuating the wounded] I remember hearing the discussion of how to remove the bodies of the pilot and co-pilot from the front of the airplane, obviously a difficult arrangement. I can't remember now how I exited the mountain—whether I went to the top or climbed back down.

Those were Bob's recollections of that day that will live forever in both of our memories. His description dovetailed so closely with what I remembered, validating all my memories. I'm certain Bob was standing right next to me as I lay on the ground after being pulled from the airplane. I too witnessed the drama of trying to bring the wire stretcher up to the helicopter two times and twice failing.

I immediately emailed Bob Bach copies of the photos of the airplane crash that Bob Ray had given me and a copy of my *Rock in the Clouds* memoir. Bob answered the same day and sent me two pictures of himself. He confessed, "That aircraft incident has always caused me some anguish in that I was not medically trained to offer any real assistance when I arrived on the scene. I've always thought that I owe that fellow I helped something more than what I was able to give on that day."

Bob Bach in VN

Bob really liked my written account of the airplane crash, telling me in later correspondence he read it three times. He answered me on Easter Sunday, 31 March 2013. He shared in writing his most poignant memory of that day:

> For many years I struggled with the image of that soldier with the broken leg and gash on his head. It is he that I, and a 1LT, tried to help that rainy October day in 1966. We were the ones who tied him in that contraption that was hoisted up by the Huey. You were but a few feet away.
>
> To this day, I regret not having the proper knowledge and tools with which to help both that soldier and you. Since my retirement and involvement with a local volunteer fire dept, I have embarked on a personal training regimen that, never again, will find me in a position of not being able to render aid to an injured person.
>
> I owe that soldier something for not being a greater help. I will try to repay him by helping other people, when in need, to the best of my ability. I hope that someday I may feel that I have made good in his eyes.

I answered him on 3 April 2013 in part:

Bob,

> I would, be pleased and honored if you would share "our" story with your children and grandchildren—and anyone else who would find it of interest. I find it absolutely amazing that the two of us should connect after all these years, and to recognize after all these years, that we were next to each other to see and experience this dramatic event in Vietnam—all after forty-seven years have passed! . . .

I think it is wonderful that you would take your experience from this event and turn it into a desire to help others in an emergency You may have noted my thoughts on the subject in my little write-up. You just can't be prepared enough for this kind of emergency.

Bob answered the same day with his last communication. In it, Bob reflected on the most jarring part of the rescue effort, his return to An Khe, and further elaborated in his final email on the impact of that event on his later life.

> . . . I remember the day of the crash there were more people taking pictures of what was going on than trying to help with the injured. To this day I do not think much of photo-journalists . . .
>
> I returned to An Khe in 1996 (thirty years after my tour) and things have changed a little—but some things had remained the same. I would not be surprised to find the aircraft still lying upside-down on that mountainside.
>
> I am involved in our local 911 and I get sworn in this week as a member of the board of trustees of the Ste. Genevieve County Health Department. I am still taking classes in emergency management as well as various classes that lend themselves to firefighting. And I am about to begin my state recertification for my EMT license which expires next year. When I took my EMT training, I was older than anyone in the class by thirty-two years; I was sixty-four years old when I got my certification. The younger people couldn't figure what an old geezer like me was doing in a classroom.

In the final email he told me where he found my email, my comment on the Aviastar Virtual Aircraft Museum webpage for the deHavilland Caribou. Bob Bach had been recovering from a hip replacement (ironic considering my hip injury) and had time to surf the web and spot my posting. He also referred me to the same website Terry had of former Caribou pilots, the C-7A Caribou Association.[10]

I will always be grateful and extremely indebted to Terry Hamby and Bob Bach for bringing more light on what happened that day in Vietnam. Following Bob's lead, I went to the page he suggested, "Vietnam War/An Khe/Hon Cong Mountain." Jim Forgette reprinted two different accounts in "Plane Crash on Hon Cong Mountain, 10/66."[11] The first account was from other air traffic controllers who were nearby at the time:

> I remember the C7A crash very well. The aircraft name was Critter 23. The two controllers on duty at the Golf Course were OP (A controller) and GH (B controller). It was severe IFR conditions in monsoon rain, and GH was controlling the aircraft. The plane was at 3000 feet when GH lost it on the radar-picture in the rain and ground clutter.
>
> GH instructed the pilot to execute a missed approach, which was responded to by the pilot, and he even asked for Hon Cong approach control radio freq. to be repeated. At 3000 feet if the pilot had just flown straight and level, he would have cleared Hon Cong (height 2750 feet).
>
> Note: there are 2 roads in An-Khe, one lead to the end of the Golf Course runway and the other to the base of Hon Cong Mountain, where it curled around the base of the mountain. The aircraft never came up on approach control radios and was seen by guys at 27 Maint. to be descending and following the wrong road, fishtailing, looking for the runway. He hit the mountain side at about 2300 feet, a totally unnecessary accident.
>
> The GCA controller GH was cleared of any wrongdoing by testimony from approach control and tower, both of whom

were monitoring the radio transmissions, and eyewitness testimony from people on the ground at 27th Maint. The weather was such that the pilot could look down and see the road but couldn't see straight ahead, so he chose to follow the wrong road, a fatal error.

The second account was pulled from a copy of the C-7A Caribou Association June 2001 Newsletter[12]—this was the group Hamby was part of, made up of former pilots from the military but also civilians who flew these STOL planes. I found the original newsletter (see end of this chapter). In this account, the writer is much more sympathetic to the plight of the pilots and reluctant to place blame.

Looking at the photos linked on Jim Forgette's page, the first two photos were taken in 1970, four years after the crash (that would describe the "peace" sign being flashed at that site).[13] I'm not sure when the next six photos were taken. Most of these I had from Bob Ray who sent them to me when he returned to action in Vietnam. Vegetation has grown around the plane, and what looks like scavenging of the airplane for metal parts has taken place. The final photo posted in the group shows the interior of the airplane, pretty much what I remember: the airplane is upside down, and the ceiling is at the bottom of the photo (see earlier account of the crash, page 65).

Two photos of the crash site in 1970, provided by Michael Payne from Jim Forgette's website

An Khe Caribou Crash

I received the following article via e-mail from Bob Dugan (Lord knows where he got it), and with the Army Otter Caribou Association's permission have reprinted it here. I'm sure that most everyone has some information about the An Khe Caribou Crash. It is very interesting to view an historic event from a very different perspective; Army vs Air Force. Ed.

Fellows: Here's a response to a letter in our Logbook (Army Otter-Caribou qtrly newsletter) regarding the 'bou crash @ AnKhe.. Thought it might be of interest.. Fred R.
— —Original Message— —-
From: BSilvey@aol.com [mailto:BSilvey@aol.com]
Sent: Friday, March 09, 2001 8:44 AM
To: wigcr@citrus.infi.net
Subject: AnKhe Crash
    The following is an example of what this association is all about - thru the Logbook and the internet we are able to find stories and event recall such as provided by Jake Hargis. While it is a sad event it is still something that occurred in our history and is important to know that heroic acts happen - but are not forgotten.

Subj: An Khe///10/04/66
Date: 3/8/01 9:41:04 AM Eastern Standard Time
From:jaketteasthsqic@worldnet.att.net (Jake Hargis)
To:t.koniarz@worldnet.att.net
CC:BSilvey@aol.com

    Read with interest, your letter on page 56 of the Logbook.
    I was the CO of the 383rd TC Det. on that day. We were right in the middle of Operation "Paul Revere" and there were floods on the Bong Son plain. The only way to get supplies in & wounded out was by air for a couple of days. We were under tremendous pressure (primarily from MG Norton & Col. Burton) to keep above 75% flyable.
    I was on the "line" when one of my troops came running up and said we had just lost an aircraft on Hon Kong. He had seen it on approach to "Golf Course" when it went in the clouds, he heard the engines scream, and then heard the aircraft hit.
    I got on my radio to the tower & they confirmed. Like an idiot, I jumped in my jeep, alone, with nothing to work with & drove to the base of Hon Kong. I encountered an MP standing on the road. He pointed up the mountain and I started to run, that lasted about twenty yards. It was nearly vertical.
    When I finally found the aircraft, it was upside

down. You could not enter initially through the front because of crash damage. The rear doors were high off the ground so it took a while to figure out how to get in. When inside, walking on the ceiling was very difficult. The front of the fuselage was split by a large mahogany tree about 1/3 of the way back. The ramp door extensions had come out of storage and flown through the cabin, & of course, the roller conveyors had done there damage also.
    There were twenty eight people on board 63-9751, 14 were dead. All were injured. Birdie was the only Army crewmember that day. He was found under a wing. He had lived through the crash (you could see where his feet had dug trying to get out) but was dead when we found him.
    All three AF crewmembers were dead. The pilot was not found for four days even though he was still in his seat. The sheet metal had folded around him.
    This was not Bird's aircraft. He had taken the day so the assigned crewchief could celebrate his birthday.
    The very brave young man with the M-16 stuck in his groin was PFC Daniel R. Madden. Most of those killed were from an artillery unit.
    We tried air-lifting direct from the crash site but the slope was too steep for rotor clearance. I still don't watch Peter Jennings on TV. He tried to interview people and litter bearers at the crash site til I had him "escorted" off.
    Reason for the crash—Golf Course air strip was being lengthened. The GCA trailor had been moved the day before...NO ONE HAD FLIGHT TESTED IT in it's new location.
    I made several return trips to the site salvaging usable parts. (there weren't many) As far as I know 63-9751 still sits on that mountain.
    Tom, I have really enjoyed the pictures with your name on them. I lost every momento in a house fire several years ago. If you know anyone with a 383rd patch, please let me know.

    What a great report -
    Jake - thanks - I will forward you comments to those on line - there must be a patch out there somewhere.
    Tom - you asked - and you got one of the best replies I think you could imagine.
Bruce

CHAPTER 25
BRINGING IT ALL TOGETHER

FROM THE FIRST TIME I had written out my memories of the crash in 1987, I continued to search for meaning and began to develop my ultimate conclusions regarding why I survived the crash. Bob Ray also survived the crash, and my reasoning involves Bob as much as it does me based on the fateful and destined intersection of our lives. I began to reveal and express my thoughts and feelings publicly in various ways, especially as they related to Bob and Peggy Ray.

FINAL MEMORIES WITH BOB AND PEGGY

In 2012, my wife Sue and I thought we would surprise Bob and Peggy by dropping in on them at their home in Sleepy Hollow during a trip through Virginia. When we approached the familiar street and house, we were shocked and dismayed to find it empty. We knocked on a neighbors' door to inquire. When no one came to the door for a long time, we returned to our car, having given up. Just then, the neighbor appeared at the door, called us back, and told us that Bob and Peggy had sold the house after the many years they had been there, and they were now both in a nursing home. But the neighbors didn't know where.

That started a scramble to get more answers, and after an internet search to locate their son Bobby, we were finally able to connect and find out what happened. Bob had gotten to a point where he needed 24-hour nursing home help, and Peggy was not doing well herself, experiencing early signs of Alzheimer's. The children moved them both into the same nursing home in Alexandria.

After this discouraging incident, I was able to contact them by phone for the next few years and talk to them (mostly Bob, although he was very difficult to understand toward the end). In the summer of 2013, I received the very sad news of Bob's death in a telephone call from his daughter Roseann. My life-long linkage to the airplane crash was now no longer with us, although by now, I had learned so much more about the plane crash and the people involved through my discoveries of the Vietnam Virtual Wall and the other contacts made.

FINDING MEANING

The funeral Mass for Bob took place at the New Chapel at Ft. Myer on 13 September 2013. I am including an appendix with Bob's obituary along with some photos of Bob—one as a young officer and one in his days as a full Colonel (Appendix E). Roseann, their daughter, asked if I would be on the altar as deacon, and she sought permission from the Catholic chaplain and received it.

I was looking forward to being at the familiar Old Post Chapel in Ft. Myer, Virginia, for the funeral, but it was in the middle of renovations. Then when I arrived at the designated chapel for the service, I hoped the Catholic priest would ask me to give the homily, but he was a bit of an "iron pants" type—bound and rigid in his time schedule and Mass ritual—and I was not able to do it.

Following the burial at Arlington, they hosted a luncheon at

Bob's favorite Army-Navy Country Club where I was able (with tears and much emotion) to give my homily. Part of my remarks follow:

It's not Bob's suffering and sacrifice that brings us here this morning. We are here to celebrate a life of hope and promise fulfilled, a life that was extended for another forty-seven years, a life of faith and courage that should be an example for all of us. The beginning of that new life for an additional forty-seven years did not begin on the afternoon of 4 October 1966 at the moment when Bob and I, both conscious, realized we had survived a horrendous airplane crash. No, it actually began about ten hours earlier that morning, when the division chaplain stuck his head into the tent we shared and asked if anyone wanted to help him celebrate Mass.

Bob and I both said yes, and so, on the top of a jeep hood being used as an altar, the priest, Bob, and I (the only ones responding to the priest's invitation) reenacted the sacrifice of Jesus Christ, and we communed with the eternal God who is the author of all life and hope and promise. I most sincerely believe that at that moment a new life was granted and began for both Bob and me.

We never know what new life will bring, but I also sincerely believe that Bob was destined to show the world what courage and endurance and sacrifice really mean. He was meant to be an example of fortitude in the face of overwhelming adversity. He was meant to be a coheir with all those who suffer and sacrifice under the banner of Jesus Christ. He was meant to be an example for all of us in the love he had for his family and friends and for his patience and acceptance of his life condition, right up to the time of his death, and finally, his patriotism and the sacrifices he willingly made for his beloved country.

I concluded my remarks with the closing stanza of the West Point alma mater which so aptly applied to Bob, and for the life of meaning and purpose he gave to all of us.

> *And when our work is done, our course on earth is run,*
> *May it be said, "Well done," Be thou at peace.*

And so to you, Bob we say, "Well done, well done." Be thou at peace. Amen.

Regretfully, when greeting Peggy Ray, although she seemed to remember Sue and I, she seemed detached due to her illness. But I was grateful to be able to share my life's deepest moment with their family.

THE IMPACT OF JESUS ON MY LIFE

For the St. Mary of the Lake's 2014 Christmas Carol Festival, I was asked to give a testimony on how Jesus has impacted my life. This allowed me to wrap up my final acceptance of the airplane crash and my understanding of my survival that day, and Bob Ray's as well.

Chris Brandt, our pastoral assistant, asked me to talk of the impact of Jesus on my life, and in doing so, I must begin with full disclosure of my complete, total, and sincere acceptance of the Real Presence in the Eucharist—my absolute belief that the Eucharist IS the body and blood of Jesus Christ. I start this way because this absolute tenet of our Catholic Faith is not universally accepted and believed by many in this world, and surprisingly, by some who call themselves Catholic.

Of course, for those of us who have crossed this threshold of absolute belief, we do not need to seek out stories or concern ourselves with the presence of Jesus in our lives—

because He IS our life—a constant and continuous part of our lives. He lives in us, and we live in Him. But every once in a while, a story emerges of how Jesus directly impacts a life, and in my particular story, I must harken back to the beginning of the day of 4 October 1966, just over forty-seven years ago, in Vietnam.

On that day, I was a staff officer of the First Air Cavalry Division, which was conducting an operation against the Vietcong in the jungles of Vietnam. The day started with a wake-up call early that morning by the division chaplain, a Catholic priest, who stuck his head in our large sleeping tent and asked if anyone wanted to attend Mass. Only two of us from the group sleeping in the tent said we would, and Major Bob Ray and I dressed quickly and walked over to the jeep, the hood of which the priest was using as an altar.

On that makeshift altar, in the presence of just Bob and I, that priest consecrated the bread and wine into the Real Presence of Jesus Christ, and we consumed the Blessed Sacrament to begin our day, to have Jesus be part of us that day. And what a day it turned out to be!

But first, I must say a few words about Maj. Bob Ray, the other person attending Mass with me that morning, because this story is as much about him as it is about me. In one of those small-world scenarios, Bob Ray and I had been freshman together at St. Lawrence University in Canton, New York. . . . Thirteen years later in 1966, Bob and I were reunited once more—this time as fellow staff officers of the 1st Air Cav Division in Vietnam. Our friendship was immediately renewed.

Bob was the Assistant G-5, and I was the Division Chemical Officer. Both being on the division staff, we operated and moved widely about the country, many times together. That's how it came to be, several weeks later, that we were sleeping in the same tent when we accepted the priest's invitation to attend Mass in the field that day. It was also destined that day that Bob and I should, individually and separately for different reasons, be called back to the division base camp at An Khe, about an hour's flight away.

We ended up sitting next to each other on the flight back in the back end of a two-engine Caribou aircraft along with twenty-seven other passengers and a flight crew of four. As we were attempting to land at the base camp in a blinding fog, the airplane flew directly into the side of Hon Cong Mountain, killing all four of the flight crew and nine of the passengers. Bob and I survived the crash; our location in the rear of the airplane was key to our survival. Time does not permit me to go into the details of this terrible, horrible crash and our truly miraculous survival, the ensuing rescue, and the medical treatment and recovery from our injuries that Bob and I experienced over the next year. Suffice to say, we both did recover from our injuries and went on to finish our Army careers.

But the story of the Vietnam war did not end for Bob and his family after he retired years later from his truly distinguished military career. About fifteen years ago, Bob was afflicted with Parkinson's Disease, a direct result of the use of Agent Orange in Vietnam. The remainder of Bob's life, along with [the lives of] all his loved ones, was defined and shaped by this progressive disease. Bob died this past September, and we buried him in Arlington Cemetery. I was privileged to say [a few words] at Bob's funeral during which I summed up the impact of Jesus on both our lives for the past forty-seven years.

I stated that there was no question in my mind that Jesus, in the Real Presence of the Eucharist on the early morning of 4 October 1966, directly impacted Bob Ray's life and mine, and I'm here this afternoon, with God's grace, forty-seven years later, to tell you about it. Amen.

THE FINAL CHAPTER

On 25 February 2017, I was trying to tidy up my attempts to "revisit" my written account of the airplane crash in Vietnam in 1966. I truly thought then I was at the end of my search. It seemed that no more could be found out about the crash, the airplane, or the people involved. I had made my best attempt to describe what happened and to relate what the impact has been on my life and the lives of other people after the crash. It felt like the final chapter took place on 30 January 2017, when we attended the funeral of Peggy Ray, Bob Ray's wife, at Arlington National Cemetery. Peggy was buried next to Bob. In the reception following, I gave my thoughts on the passing of Peggy Ray, and those written remarks embodied my final witness to all these events.

Thoughts on the Passing of Peggy Ray

At my age, and perhaps because of my deaconate ministry, I have had more than my share of reflecting on the passing of relatives and friends in the past few years. And I do this reflecting by writing down my thoughts at the computer keyboard and electronically storing all my efforts in a file called "Thoughts on the Passing of . . ." My file contains my thoughts of the passing of my brother about a year ago and his wife a few years before that. I have an entry in the file of my thoughts on the passing of Peggy's husband, my dear friend, Bob, which I shared at the luncheon following his funeral. Recently, I wrote a reflection on my thoughts on the passing of Peggy Ray. I feel privileged and honored that you have asked me to share these thoughts with you.

I continue to be a witness to a story that began a long time ago in 1952 when two young men became friends living at the same college dorm for that school year. They separated at the end of that year and went their own ways for the next thirteen, both marrying, raising families, and pursuing military careers.

Fate would have them meet again in 1966 in Vietnam, and shortly afterwards, they experienced together an incredible, life-altering event, a violent airplane crash which they both survived and where a number of others in that airplane were killed. This sharp confrontation with death defined in a truly memorable way their relationship and the relationship between their families for the rest of all their lives.

The story I witnessed that began with Bob Ray in 1952 continued for the remainder of our military careers and well afterwards until Bob's death in 2013. Today, my witness continues with the recent death of Bob's wife, Peggy Ray, and those intervening years since the airplane crash in 1966. It tells of their families getting to know each other in a bond of friendship during those years, drawn together by relief and thanksgiving for survival and a sincere recognition of the source and power of the "how" and "why" of that survival. My witness, shared by both Bob and Peggy, is that our lives were spared that October day in 1966 by the holy communion, the Eucharist, that Bob and I received together in the field just hours before the crash.

We built on that recognition during the intervening years when we lived close to each other in Annandale, and their home in Sleepy Hollow became a place of visiting and close friendship and many dinners. We watched our children grow and expand into families of their own. This time was also marked by Bob's Parkinson's disease, the war that never ended for Bob and Peggy Ray, the incredible battle he and Peggy fought against that illness for all those years.

My witness is that of small-sized Peggy Ray holding onto good-sized Bob Ray, walking backwards and supporting him as Bob struggled to move about the house during the later stages of his illness. My witness is that of a wife who was loving and selfless and dedicated to her husband and her family. My witness is that of a true Army wife who experienced all the highs and lows of following her husband's Army career. She did it all with such grace and confidence. She was a truly great lady in every respect.

But my witness to this story cannot, will not, and does not end with Peggy Ray's death. So, as long as God gives me eyes and ears to witness, I will continue to proclaim the value of dedicated service, the special love between a man and his wife, and the beauty and meaning of lives well lived. So, be at peace, Peggy Ray. Be at peace, Bob and Peggy Ray. It has been a special privilege of mine to have been a witness to all this. You gave us a great example to live by. Well done. Well done. Amen.

EPILOGUE
THE STORY OF A WAR NEVER ENDS

"Over the years, I've learned to describe this experience in a shorthand way: Every day is Christmas!"

THOUGHTS OF THE WAR and the airplane crash are never far from my mind. I am frequently asked about my feelings and outlook after having survived an airplane crash. Depending on the circumstances of the conversation, I prepared, over time, three responses to their queries. If the situation requires a quick, snappy comeback, I reply, "Don't try this at home!" On other occasions, I quip, "If you're making a bucket list, forget this one!" But when I really needed to be serious in responding, I declared my true feelings, which are "Every day is Christmas!" Even when people solicitously asked me, "How ya doing?" I never hesitated to answer, "Every day is Christmas!" This sober conviction had become a part of my life, and I always express it with sincerity.

It was a process of years, from 1987 to 2021, that I added to what I knew and contemplated writing a book. I thought I had everything I would find in 2017 as I put my final pages together after Peggy Ray's passing and packed them away once more. Then, my editor began piecing it all together for the full manuscript of this book. In doing some additional checking on my website references, she turned up even more information to document the "revisited" part of the story.

Two additional individuals responded to my inquiry on the de Havilland website[14] *years* after I had posted the request in the "Comments" section on 4 October 2011. I had simply failed to follow up checking this website in the intervening nine years. For example, on 3 June 2016, Shawn Giefing had responded to my post as follows:

Shawn Giefing . . . 06.03.2016 07:13

My papaw was also one of the survivors of the C7 tail wing 63-9751 crash on HK mountain. His name was Elmer Dale Bass. Any other survivors or people who remember his name feel free to contact me. He passed away March of 2015. I've been trying to contact any friends that served with him to hear stories of my papaw and the brave men he served beside. God Bless our troops and welcome home. To the ones who have fallen may they forever rest in peace as the heroes they are.

I immediately sent the following reply to Shawn:

Joe Tedeschi . . . 08.08.2020 Re: Shawn Giefing

Hi Shawn, I'm so sorry I did not follow up my comment back in 2011, and to look for comments in reply. Just to find another name of a person also in the crash and survived it is so rewarding. I send my sincere condolences on the loss of your papaw. I would have liked to have known him and to contact him to get his story. I'm in the process of writing an account of the crash, and I have names of 5 of the people who survived the crash. Please try to contact me, even after 4 years since you posted your comment. My e-mail is t . . .@verizon. net . . . I've gathered a large amount of material concerning the crash which I would be happy to share with you. I sincerely hope we can connect.

Joe Tedeschi

Eventually Shawn was able to get back to me. He told me he had joined the army as an infantry soldier, just like his grandfather, and his delay in answering was due to an overseas deployment that made it difficult to maintain even electronic communications. Shawn, so proud of his "papaw" and the service he gave to the nation, followed in line with the many heroes who step up to man our armed forces. I know his papaw, in turn, would be so proud of him for the service he is now performing.

Another person who responded to my post in the intervening time on 17 October 2014 was Andrea Webster, and her reply really piqued my excitement. She posted:

Andrea Webster . . . 17.10.2014 21:32

Mr. Joseph Tedeschi, my grandfather was also aboard that plane when it crashed. It has been years since your post but my father and I would love to get in touch with you! Please email us if you can at a . . . @gmail.com.

THE CARIBOU PILOT

I knew from the information gathered on the Vietnam Virtual Wall that Captain Webster was one of the pilots. In subsequent communications, I was to find out he was the pilot, and I now had contact with his family. I felt having a connection with any one of the air crew's families would be phenomenal for the book. My comprehension and search for meaning of the crash would reach a degree of completeness if I knew their side of the story and how it impacted their lives. Seeing her message six years after her post, I responded immediately to Andrea and waited anxiously to get a reply. I did not have much hope of getting one.

Hi Andrea,

Certainly hope this email gets through to you on this "dated" email address. I responded to your 2014 comment to my 2011 comment on the DeHaviland Caribou web site as follows:

Joe Tedeschi, e-mail, 08.08.2020 Andrea Webster

Hi Andrea, Please see my reply to Shawn Giefing above whose [grand]father survived the crash. My thoughts and sentiments go out to you and your father as well. Your grandfather was the co-pilot, and I have a copy of his panel from the Virtual VN Wall. Please, after all these years, we must try to get in contact and I will share with you the information I've gathered so far. Perhaps you might have some new information I could use in my written account I'm currently in the process of writing. The VN war will never end until we tell the last story.

To my surprise and absolute delight, I received a reply just two days later, not from Andrea, but from Captain Webster's son Chris. This began an exchange of emails with Chris, the body of which speaks for itself and tells its own story. The flow of the emails does so much in complementing and completing my own story, and for this reason, I include them in their entirety.

From: Christopher Webster <c . . . @gmail.com>
To: t . . . @verizon.net; Andrea Webster <a . . . @gmail.com>
Sent: Mon, Aug 10, 2020 8:24 am
Subject: RE: Fwd: Caribou Crash 1966

Hi Joe. My name is Chris Webster, and I'm Andrea's father and David Webster's son.

Thanks for all your work investigating and writing about this crash; I look forward to reading it.

As a point of clarification, my father, Capt. David O'Neal Webster, was the pilot of the airplane, not the co-pilot.

Sincerely,
Chris Webster

Another incredible discovery, after all these years, after I thought that I had exhausted all my resources! I responded to Chris right away seeking more information.

From: Joseph R. Tedeschi <t . . . @verizon.net>
To: c . . . @gmail.com
Sent: Mon, Aug 10, 2020 12:15 pm
Subject: Re: Caribou Crash 1966

Hi Chris and Andrea!

I continue to be overwhelmed by the way in which things are falling into place in my attempts to clarify (in writing) the airplane crash on 4 Oct 66—in which your father died, and I survived as a passenger. Thank you for the correction. I made the mistake of thinking that Capt. Bissaillon was the pilot because his name was listed first in the names of the flight crew posted on the VN Virtual Wall in "A Note from the Virtual Wall." Are you familiar with the VN Virtual Wall? I really began my search for more details of the crash after I first discovered the web site in 2010. Things have snow balled since then, and I have been able to gather a significant amount of material concerning the details of the crash, personnel involved, witnesses to the crash scene, etc. Just recently, I thought I had enough to write a book, and I have engaged an editor to help me pull it together. Do you have any photos or material that might be included?

Since I am just at the beginning to work with my editor, my manuscript is in a very early stage, but as it progresses, I would be privileged to share it with you. In the meantime, I would be happy to provide you with some of the material I've gathered and some of my earlier attempts to write an account.

I can't tell you how touched and anxious I am to share this story with you and Andrea. I will always have the VN war and the crash in the back of my mind as it must be for you as well. As I posted in my note to Andrea, "The VN war will never end until we tell the last story." Our story of the crash may never be "completed," but I think sharing it will help.

Joe

From: Christopher Webster <c . . . @gmail.com>
To: Joseph R. Tedeschi <t . . . @verizon.net>
Sent: Mon, Aug 10, 2020 8:53 pm
Subject: Re: Caribou Crash 1966

Joe, I didn't realize that you were one of the survivors of the crash. I've often thought what a terrible day that must have been for you guys; first being wounded on the battlefield then in an airplane crash.

There is another note of clarification; Bissaillon was a Lieutenant, not a Captain.

I eagerly look forward to reading your book and am happy to provide anything I can, just let me know what you would like to have. If you're willing, please send me the manuscript when it's ready.

I've never spoken to a survivor of the crash, just to a few eye witnesses.

Chris

His note about Bissaillon illustrates a perspective needed when browsing those posted on the Virtual Vietnam Wall. Their rank sometimes was promoted after death, so the entries show their final "rank," which may differ from what others knew in the field. There was also some contradictory information in the redacted official crash investigation papers I finally got to see after my first full draft of this book was complete, and the lead papers show Bissaillon as the captain that day, Webster as copilot, and later in the records the roles are reversed. So the posting on the Vietnam Virtual Wall probably used the first parts of these records.

From: Joseph R. Tedeschi <t . . . @verizon.net>
Sent: Tuesday, August 11, 2020 6:14 PM
To: c . . . @gmail.com
Subject: Re: Caribou Crash 1966

Hi Chris,

Allow me to send you a "first cut" I did back in 1999 to begin writing an account of the crash. As you will note, I did not have many details of the crash at that time. Since then, thanks to the Virtual VN Wall, I have learned so much more that I think I can put a book together. Please give me a reaction to my early written account. You certainly are a key person that I want to reach and get your perspective on the tragedy that took place 54 years ago.

Joe

To: Joseph R. Tedeschi <t . . . @verizon.net>
Sent: Wed, Aug 12, 2020 10:55 am
Subject: RE: Caribou Crash 1966

Joe,

I've just finished reading your account; thank you!

It is a compelling story and certainly provides me with a different perspective of the crash and the aftermath.

I believe that you were at Hammond when you boarded the airplane. Can you describe it to me? Your account indicates that it was not improved, and I'd love to hear a first-hand account of both Hammond and An Khe (especially An Khe!).

I'm also very interested in what you have learned about the crash since this writing. It is my understanding that, while the cause of the crash has never been determined with certainty, the prevailing theory is that the Air Force was preparing to bring in a larger airplane (the C5), and in preparation for making the runway larger, they had to move the radar trailer. They hadn't had time to recalibrate it when Dad's flight arrived, and he was vectored in using faulty information.

I understand that the air traffic controller was court martialed but found not guilty. The poor guy was just doing his job, and I'll bet he had nightmares for years afterward over that incident.

Lastly, can I share your story with my brothers and daughters? I'm sure they'd love to read it.

Chris

From: Joseph R. Tedeschi <t . . . @verizon.net>
Date: 8/12/20 13:37 (GMT-05:00)
To: c . . . @gmail.com
Subject: Re: Caribou Crash 1966

Hi Chris,

Your positive response to my initial written account is very important to me. Thank you for that. Yes, we were at Hammond. I wrote the first account over thirty years after the crash, and I'm glad I did because memory does fade, and my memory back then was better than it is now! I don't remember too much about Hammond except for the airstrip and a few other details. The airfield at An Khe (they called it the "Golf Course") was a good size. I'll see what I can dig up with more descriptive information about An Khe. I have two accounts of the crash I retrieved from the Caribou Association web site. I plan to use them in my book. Check them out at https://www.freewebs.com/jim4jet/ c7acaribou.htm. These are two views of what happened. You provide a third which I had not heard.

By all means, share the account with your daughters and brothers. As the manuscript evolves with my editor, I will share as much as I can with you. I hope to finish by the end of the year, so I'll be in contact to share it with you. If you have any info, photos, etc., and would be willing to have me include them in my book, please let me know.

Joe

Air Gas Station Saves 7 Jets

A KC-135 "Flying Gas Sttion" from Homestead Air Force Base this week was credited with saving seven supersonic jet fighters dangerously low on fuel at Mac-Dill AFB near Tampa.

Air Force officials said the 407th Air Refueling Squadron's KC-135, piloted by Capt. David Webster, was on a scheduled B-52 refueling run when an F-84 jet fighter with faulty landing gear crash-landed on the MacDill field runway.

Seven 1,800-mph F4C Phanton jets, circling the field to land, were directed to the KC-135 to tank up while the crippled jet was being towed from the runway.

★ ★ ★

Capt. Webster's flight experience before Vietnam

From: Christopher Webster <c . . . @gmail.com>

To: Joseph R. Tedeschi <t . . . @verizon.net>

Sent: Wed, Aug 12, 2020 3:15 pm

Subject: Re: Caribou Crash 1966

I can tell you that Dad flew refuelers for SAC before Vietnam. He trained on, and briefly flew the B29 (converted to a refueling airplane), then he flew the KC97 in Montana, then was transferred to Miami, FL, where he was upgraded to a jet[15] in the KC 135. From there, he was sent to Vietnam, where he flew the Caribou.

I think it's obvious that I wouldn't want Dad to be reflected in a poor light in the book. He was an excellent pilot, which is why he was there. That is, with the Air Force taking over fixed wing aircraft, they wanted their best pilots there at the takeover to make a good impression.

The transition for this Army/Air Force agreement became official on 1 Jan 1967, I believe, and was called the Johnson-McConnell agreement.

The Army called the C-7A Caribou the CV-2, and since the crash occurred in 1966 and the airplane had Army markings, it would have been (technically speaking) a CV-2, not the Air Force designation C-7A Caribou. Also, while Dad was career Air Force (seventeen years when he died), he was temporarily assigned to the Army. That would have changed in 1967 when the AF took over that airplane, of course.

So, while Dad was new "In Country" and new to the "'bou," he wasn't a "young," inexperienced pilot.

I don't mean to belabor the point. I just want to understand how he will be portrayed before I supply photos and more information about him for publication.

From: "Joseph R. Tedeschi" <t . . . @verizon.net>
Date: 8/13/20 16:46 (GMT-05:00)
To: c . . . @gmail.com
Subject: Re: Caribou Crash 1966

Dear Chris,

I give you my solemn vow that I would NEVER portray your father in the manner you describe. Rather, I would portray him (if I decide to use more in-depth information about other individuals involved in the crash) as the dedicated, highly professional airman that he was, and one of the innumerable Heroes that sacrificed their lives for our country. I plan to disclose the two "reports" of the incident from the Caribou Association website. Also, I plan to use the account written up in the 1967 issue of "Aviation Digest," which describes in more detail the circumstances prevalent that day, and which includes quotes from the official inquiry. I can send you a copy if you would like. I don't see anything derogatory of your father in these accounts of the crash. I do give a lot of in-depth attention to Col Bob Ray (sitting next to me in the airplane) in my account because of the most unusual circumstances that placed us in adjoining seats. The more I learn of others involved in the crash, the more I am inclined to add these profiles to my manuscript. In that light, the more I know about your father, the more I would be pleased and honored to add in the most positive way to my story. That's the only reason for asking for more information from you. Whatever I write, I will most certainly send to you beforehand and get your approval. I plan to do this for the Ray family as well.

Please believe me when I say that my account of the crash is meant to tell the story of just one of the tragedies that took place during VN war, and in doing so, to honor and commemorate all those who died and were injured that day. My story has no place for finger pointing in any way. When it's finished, I think you will find it to be a compassionate account of all the people involved in the crash, the impact on their lives and their families. You will see, as well, my lifelong attempts to rationalize my survival, and the spiritual conclusion that has consoled me.

Joe

From: Christopher Webster <c . . . @gmail.com>
To: Joseph R. Tedeschi <t . . . @verizon.net>
Sent: Thu, Aug 13, 2020 4:56 pm
Subject: Re: Caribou Crash 1966

Thanks, Joe. I appreciate your fairness.

I'm also sure that if Dad had survived the crash, he would be the first to say that he screwed up, and his conscience would be forever troubled.

Please tell me what you would like from me for the book, and I'll send it along.

By the way, I live in the Atlanta area. If you're close, it would be great to get together for dinner.

Thanks for telling this story for us all,

Chris

P.S. My three brothers really liked your book.

From: Joseph R. Tedeschi <t . . . @verizon.net>
To: <c . . . @gmail.com>
Sent: Fri, Aug 14, 2020 5:05 pm
Subject: Re: Caribou Crash 1966

Chris,

    I'll talk to my editor to see if we want to profile in detail anyone else in the crash (other than Bob Ray). I'm inclined to do so since we have so little info of the backgrounds of anyone else in the crash. It's something I would like to do for your father. In that light, whatever bio info (similar to what you sent me earlier, establishing that he had plenty of flying experience over a wide range of aircraft), and photos you have, would be welcome, and we'll see how we can weave that into the manuscript.

    Thanks for the dinner offer. My travel days (I did quite a bit in earlier times) are somewhat constrained these days, but if I do get down your way, I'll take you up on the offer. I recall the "seasoned travelers" quip about the Atlanta airport: If you have been sentenced to hell, you must travel through the Atlanta airport on the way! Must admit that I did have some frustrating layovers there, and remarkable dashes on the connecting train between flights. I live in Medford, N.J., and I extend the same invitation to you if you should be in this area. Now for the balancing quip: When you give travel directions in New Jersey, you always use the exits off the Jersey Turnpike as reference. I live off exit #4!

    So very pleased your brothers liked what I've already written.

Joe

From: <c...@gmail.com>
To: Joseph R. Tedeschi <t . . . @verizon.net>
Sent: Fri, Aug 21, 2020 4:04 pm
Subject: RE: Caribou Crash 1966

Hi Joe,

Sorry it has taken so long for me to get this to you. This is my Dad, Capt. David O. Webster USAF. This picture was taken in Florida on moving day. He had received his orders to Vietnam, and the family was moving my mom and the four of us (four boys) to Arizona to be near her family.

What else can I get to you?

Chris

Capt. Webster and three of his four sons

I wanted to answer the following to Chris:

No, Chris, it's not what you can get for me; it's what can I get for you and your family. I survived the crash and have spent a great deal of time and energy thinking about it. Your family lost your dad, and the pain it must have caused is just too much for me to imagine.

The flood of memories that come to me when I see the picture of your dad and his boys on moving day brings back the pain I felt and share with you when I had to leave my family at just about the same time. I, too, had to move my family from Alabama to Rhode Island just prior to my leaving for Vietnam. I moved them for the same reason—to be near family.

I suspect your dad and family were experiencing the tremendous turmoil and disruption in your lives at about the same time as we were. I can only imagine the path of destiny that brought us together on 4 October 1966 as pilot and passenger on that Caribou aircraft. Your dad and your family will be forever linked, in a special way, to me and my family, as we share the terrible burden of what happened that day.

But to my great dismay, I found out three weeks after sending him the manuscript that he had gone into the hospital about that time with Covid-19 and lost his battle against the disease. I was able to talk with his daughter, Andrea. She said she had read the book to him before he passed, and she was certain he would approve of her grandfather's part in it.

ACKNOWLEDGEMENTS

MY BOOK AND THE story behind it would not have come about without some genuine help and understanding. I acknowledge first the creator God, the Catholic Church, and the gift of faith which has always informed and sustained me. I thank Sue, my precious wife and truly best friend for sixty-four years, who lived all this with me. To my daughters, Susanne and Marly, my sister, Theresa, and all my extended family and friends, thank you for your love and incredible support. I'm especially indebted to the Bob and Peggy Ray family and the destined linkage which brought us together. I am also forever appreciative of West Point and the army which became my life for so many years and molded that youngster searching for a future of something good and made me who I am.

I am indebted in a special way to my editor, Shauna Perez, who became my mentor, guide, and friend in taking me through the maze as a new author trying to write a book. Finally, to Koehler Books and staff, thank you for accepting my manuscript and giving me a platform to tell my story.

APPENDIX A
VIRTUAL VIETNAM WALL
MEMORIALS

I AM INCLUDING THE following pages to honor the men who died in the Critter 23 crash that day. The Virtual Vietnam Wall is maintained by volunteers who work to help honor and remember their fallen brothers. In the event that this valiant Virtual Memorial ever gets taken down, I wanted to be sure to remember and honor them all here.

David O'Neil Webster

```
ON THE WALL:        Panel 11E Line 47
This page Copyright© 1997-2018 www.VirtualWall.org Ltd.
PERSONAL DATA:
  Home of Record:   Phoenix, AZ
  Date of birth:    08/12/1932
MILITARY DATA:
  Service Branch:   United States Air Force
  Grade at loss:    O3
  Rank:             Captain
Promotion Note:     None
  ID No:            3037851
  MOS:              1115: Pilot, Tactical Aircraft,
                    (various)
  Length Service:   16
  Unit:             6252ND OPS SQDN, 7TH AF
CASUALTY DATA:
  Start Tour:       08/16/1966
  Incident Date:    10/04/1966
  Casualty Date:    10/04/1966
  Status Date:      Not Applicable
  Status Change:    Not Applicable
  Age at Loss:      34
  Location:         Binh Dinh Province, South Vietnam
  Remains:          Body recovered
  Repatriated:      Not Applicable
  Identified:       Not Applicable
  Casualty Type:    Hostile, died outright
  Casualty Reason:  Fixed Wing - Pilot
  Casualty Detail:  Air loss or crash over land
  URL: /VirtualWall.org/dw/WebsterD001a.htm
  Data accessed:    9/30/2020
```

THE VIRTUAL WALL ®   www.VirtualWall.org

David O'Neil Webster

Captain
6252ND OPS SQDN, 7TH AF
United States Air Force
Phoenix, Arizona
August 12, 1932 to October 04, 1966
DAVID O WEBSTER **is on the Wall at** Panel 11E, Line 47
See the full profile **or** name rubbing **for David Webster**

Francis Henry Bissaillon

ON THE WALL: **Panel 11E Line 43**

This page Copyright© 1997-2018 www.VirtualWall.org Ltd.

PERSONAL DATA:
    Home of Record: Williamstown, MA
    Date of birth: 05/23/1938
MILITARY DATA:
    Service Branch: United States Air Force
    Grade at loss: O2
    Rank: Posthumous Promotion as indicated
Promotion Note: None
    ID No: 3135622
    MOS: 1115: Pilot, Tactical Aircraft,
                        (various)
    Length Service: 03
    Unit: 6252ND OPS SQDN, 7TH AF
CASUALTY DATA:
    Start Tour: 08/08/1966
    Incident Date: 10/04/1966
    Casualty Date: 10/04/1966
    Status Date: Not Applicable
    Status Change: Not Applicable
    Age at Loss: 28
    Location: Binh Dinh Province, South Vietnam
    Remains: Body recovered
    Repatriated: Not Applicable
    Identified: Not Applicable
    Casualty Type: Hostile, died outright
    Casualty Reason: Fixed Wing - Crew
    Casualty Detail: Air loss or crash over land
    URL: /VirtualWall.org/db/BissaillonFH01a.htm
    Data accessed: 10/1/2020

THE VIRTUAL WALL ®   www.VirtualWall.org

Print This Page   Close This Page
Page template 10/09/2015

Francis Henry Bissaillon

Captain
6252ND OPS SQDN, 7TH AF
United States Air Force
Williamstown, Massachusetts
May 23, 1938 to October 04, 1966
FRANCIS H BISSAILLON is on the Wall at Panel 11E, Line 43
See the full profile or name rubbing for Francis Bissaillon

Daniel Paul Marlowe

ON THE WALL: Panel 11E Line 45

This page Copyright© 1997-2018 www.VirtualWall.org Ltd.

PERSONAL DATA:
  Home of Record: San Antonio, TX
  Date of birth: 08/14/1928

MILITARY DATA:
  Service Branch: United States Air Force
  Grade at loss: E5
  Rank: Staff Sergeant
Promotion Note: None
  ID No: 14198360
  MOS: -----: Not Recorded
  Length Service: 14
  Unit: 6252ND OPS SQDN, 7TH AF

CASUALTY DATA:
  Start Tour: 09/21/1966
  Incident Date: 10/04/1966
  Casualty Date: 10/04/1966
  Status Date: Not Applicable
  Status Change: Not Applicable
  Age at Loss: 38
  Location: Binh Dinh Province, South Vietnam
  Remains: Body recovered
  Repatriated: Not Applicable
  Identified: Not Applicable
  Casualty Type: Hostile, died outright
  Casualty Reason: Fixed Wing - Crew
  Casualty Detail: Air loss or crash over land
  URL: /VirtualWall.org/dm/MarloweDP01a.htm
  Data accessed: 8/26/2020

THE VIRTUAL WALL ®   www.VirtualWall.org

Daniel Paul Marlowe
Staff Sergeant
6252ND OPS SQDN, 7TH AF
United States Air Force
San Antonio, Texas
August 14, 1928 to October 04, 1966
DANIEL P MARLOWE is on the Wall at Panel 11E, Line 45
See the full profile or name rubbing for Daniel Marlowe

John Thomas Bird

ON THE WALL: Panel 11E Line 43

This page Copyright© 1997-2018 www.VirtualWall.org Ltd.

PERSONAL DATA:
  Home of Record: Summit, NJ
  Date of birth: 03/14/1944

MILITARY DATA:
  Service Branch: Army of the United States
  Grade at loss: E4
  Rank: Specialist Four
Promotion Note: None
  ID No: 51544647
  MOS: -----: Not Recorded
  Length Service: 01
  Unit: 17TH AVN CO, 1ST CAV DIV, USARV

CASUALTY DATA:
  Start Tour: 01/08/1966
  Incident Date: 10/04/1966
  Casualty Date: 10/04/1966
  Status Date: Not Applicable
  Status Change: Not Applicable
  Age at Loss: 22
  Location: Binh Dinh Province, South Vietnam
  Remains: Body recovered
  Repatriated: Not Applicable
  Identified: Not Applicable
  Casualty Type: Non-hostile, died while missing
  Casualty Reason: Fixed Wing - Crew
  Casualty Detail: Air loss or crash over land
  URL: /VirtualWall.org/db/BirdJT01a.htm
  Data accessed: 8/25/2020

THE VIRTUAL WALL ®   www.VirtualWall.org

John Thomas Bird

Specialist Four
17TH AVN CO, 1ST CAV DIV, USARV
Army of the United States
Summit, New Jersey
March 14, 1944 to October 04, 1966
JOHN T BIRD **is on the Wall at** Panel 11E, Line 43
See the full profile **or** name rubbing **for John Bird**

Johnnie Lincoln Daniel

ON THE WALL: **Panel 11E Line 44**

This page Copyright© 1997-2018 www.VirtualWall.org Ltd.

PERSONAL DATA:
  Home of Record: Johnston, SC
  Date of birth: 04/17/1931

MILITARY DATA:
  Service Branch: Army of the United States
  Grade at loss: O3
  Rank: Captain
Promotion Note: None
  ID No: O4029119
  MOS: 6401: Unknown MOS
  Length Service: 12
  Unit: HHC, 1ST BDE, 1ST CAV DIV, USARV

CASUALTY DATA:
  Start Tour: 03/23/1966
  Incident Date: 10/04/1966
  Casualty Date: 10/04/1966
  Status Date: Not Applicable
  Status Change: Not Applicable
  Age at Loss: 35
  Location: Binh Dinh Province, South Vietnam
  Remains: Body recovered
  Repatriated: Not Applicable
  Identified: Not Applicable
  Casualty Type: Non-hostile, died while missing
  Casualty Reason: Fixed Wing - Noncrew
  Casualty Detail: Air loss or crash over land
  URL: /VirtualWall.org/dd/DanielJL03a.htm
  Data accessed: 8/26/2020

THE VIRTUAL WALL ®   www.VirtualWall.org

Print This Page   Close This Page
Page template 10/09/2015

Johnnie Lincoln Daniel

Captain
HHC, 1ST BDE, 1ST CAV DIV, USARV
Army of the United States
Johnston, South Carolina
April 17, 1931 to October 04, 1966
JOHNNIE L DANIEL **is on the Wall at** Panel 11E, Line 44
See the full profile **or** name rubbing **for Johnnie Daniel**

Kenneth Wade West

ON THE WALL: **Panel 11E Line 48**

This page Copyright© 1997-2018 www.VirtualWall.org Ltd.

PERSONAL DATA:
  Home of Record: Jacksonville, FL
  Date of birth: 06/26/1943

MILITARY DATA:
  Service Branch: Army of the United States
  Grade at loss: O2
  Rank: First Lieutenant
Promotion Note: None
  ID No: OF106037
  MOS: 71193: Field Artillery Unit
                   Commander (Airborne Qual)
  Length Service: 00
  Unit: B BTRY, 2ND BN, 19TH ARTILLERY, 1ST
                   CAV DIV, USARV

CASUALTY DATA:
  Start Tour: 08/04/1966
  Incident Date: 10/04/1966
  Casualty Date: 10/04/1966
  Status Date: Not Applicable
  Status Change: Not Applicable
  Age at Loss: 23
  Location: Binh Dinh Province, South Vietnam
  Remains: Body recovered
  Repatriated: Not Applicable
  Identified: 10/07/1966
  Casualty Type: Non-hostile, died while missing
  Casualty Reason: Fixed Wing - Noncrew
  Casualty Detail: Air loss or crash over land
  URL: /VirtualWall.org/dw/WestKW01a.htm
  Data accessed: 8/26/2020

THE VIRTUAL WALL ®   www.VirtualWall.org

[Print This Page]   [Close This Page]
Page template 10/09/2015

Find A Name ▼   The Virtual Wall® ▼   This Memorial Page ▼

Kenneth Wade West

First Lieutenant
B BTRY, 2ND BN, 19TH ARTILLERY, 1ST CAV DIV, USARV
Army of the United States
Jacksonville, Florida
June 26, 1943 to October 04, 1966
KENNETH W WEST is on the Wall at Panel 11E, Line 48
See the full profile or name rubbing for Kenneth West

Armando Ramos

ON THE WALL: **Panel 11E Line 46**

This page Copyright© 1997-2018 www.VirtualWall.org Ltd.

PERSONAL DATA:
  Home of Record: Santurce, PR
  Date of birth: 01/01/1921
MILITARY DATA:
  Service Branch: Army of the United States
  Grade at loss: E7
  Rank: Sergeant First Class
Promotion Note: None
  ID No: 30403205
  MOS: 05B40: Radio Operator
  Length Service: 20
  Unit: A CO, 13TH SIG BN, 1ST CAV DIV, USARV
CASUALTY DATA:
  Start Tour: 12/13/1965
  Incident Date: 10/04/1966
  Casualty Date: 10/04/1966
  Status Date: Not Applicable
  Status Change: Not Applicable
  Age at Loss: 45
  Location: Binh Dinh Province, South Vietnam
  Remains: Body recovered
  Repatriated: Not Applicable
  Identified: 10/07/1966
  Casualty Type: Non-hostile, died while missing
  Casualty Reason: Fixed Wing - Noncrew
  Casualty Detail: Air loss or crash over land
  URL: /VirtualWall.org/dr/RamosAx01a.htm
  Data accessed: 8/26/2020

THE VIRTUAL WALL ®   www.VirtualWall.org

Print This Page   Close This Page
Page template 10/09/2015

Find A Name ▼   The Virtual Wall® ▼   This Memorial Page ▼

Armando Ramos
Sergeant First Class
A CO, 13TH SIG BN, 1ST CAV DIV, USARV
Army of the United States
Santurce, Puerto Rico
January 01, 1921 to October 04, 1966
ARMANDO RAMOS is on the Wall at Panel 11E, Line 46
See the full profile or name rubbing for Armando Ramos

Richard Michael Prociv

ON THE WALL: **Panel 11E Line 46**

This page Copyright© 1997-2018 www.VirtualWall.org Ltd.

PERSONAL DATA:
  Home of Record: Salt Lake City, UT
  Date of birth: 03/30/1934
MILITARY DATA:
  Service Branch: Army of the United States
  Grade at loss: E6
  Rank: Staff Sergeant
Promotion Note: None
  ID No: 28726179
  MOS: 71P4P: Flight Operations Coordinator
                  (Airborne Qual)
  Length Service: 10
  Unit: HHC, 1ST BDE, 1ST CAV DIV, USARV
CASUALTY DATA:
  Start Tour: 08/22/1966
  Incident Date: 10/04/1966
  Casualty Date: 10/04/1966
  Status Date: Not Applicable
  Status Change: Not Applicable
  Age at Loss: 32
  Location: Binh Dinh Province, South Vietnam
  Remains: Body recovered
  Repatriated: Not Applicable
  Identified: 10/07/2012
  Casualty Type: Non-hostile, died while missing
  Casualty Reason: Fixed Wing - Noncrew
  Casualty Detail: Air loss or crash over land
  URL: /VirtualWall.org/dp/ProcivRM01a.htm
  Data accessed: 8/26/2020

THE VIRTUAL WALL ®   www.VirtualWall.org

Find A Name ▼   The Virtual Wall® ▼   This Memorial Page ▼

Richard Michael Prociv

Staff Sergeant
HHC, 1ST BDE, 1ST CAV DIV, USARV
Army of the United States
Salt Lake City, Utah
March 30, 1934 to October 04, 1966
RICHARD M PROCIV **is on the Wall at** Panel 11E, Line 46
See the full profile **or** name rubbing **for Richard Prociv**

Homer Lee Pickett

ON THE WALL: **Panel 11E Line 46**

This page Copyright© 1997-2018 www.VirtualWall.org Ltd.

PERSONAL DATA:
  Home of Record: Oklahoma City, OK
  Date of birth: 11/16/1935

MILITARY DATA:
  Service Branch: Army of the United States
  Grade at loss: E5
  Rank: Sergeant
Promotion Note: None
  ID No: 18490772
  MOS: 13B40: Cannon Crewmember
  Length Service: 10
  Unit: B BTRY, 1ST BN, 21ST ARTILLERY, 1ST
                     CAV DIV, USARV

CASUALTY DATA:
  Start Tour: 05/08/1966
  Incident Date: 10/04/1966
  Casualty Date: 10/04/1966
  Status Date: Not Applicable
  Status Change: Not Applicable
  Age at Loss: 30
  Location: Binh Dinh Province, South Vietnam
  Remains: Body recovered
  Repatriated: Not Applicable
  Identified: 10/06/1966
  Casualty Type: Non-hostile, died while missing
  Casualty Reason: Fixed Wing - Noncrew
  Casualty Detail: Air loss or crash over land
  URL: /VirtualWall.org/dp/PickettHL01a.htm
  Data accessed: 8/25/2020

THE VIRTUAL WALL ®   www.VirtualWall.org

Print This Page   Close This Page
Page template 10/09/2015

Homer Lee Pickett

Sergeant
B BTRY, 1ST BN, 21ST ARTILLERY, 1ST CAV DIV, USARV
Army of the United States
Oklahoma City, Oklahoma
November 16, 1935 to October 04, 1966
HOMER L PICKETT **is on the Wall at** Panel 11E, Line 46
See the full profile **or** name rubbing **for Homer Pickett**

James Garris Litts

ON THE WALL: **Panel 11E Line 45**

This page Copyright© 1997-2018 www.VirtualWall.org Ltd.

PERSONAL DATA:
    Home of Record: Bushkill, PA
    Date of birth: 02/01/1947
MILITARY DATA:
    Service Branch: Army of the United States
    Grade at loss: E3
    Rank: Private First Class
Promotion Note: None
    ID No: 14917563
    MOS: -----: Not Recorded
    Length Service: 00
    Unit: HHC, 8TH ENG BN, 1ST CAV DIV, USARV
CASUALTY DATA:
    Start Tour: 01/06/1966
    Incident Date: 10/04/1966
    Casualty Date: 10/04/1966
    Status Date: Not Applicable
    Status Change: Not Applicable
    Age at Loss: 19
    Location: Binh Dinh Province, South Vietnam
    Remains: Body recovered
    Repatriated: Not Applicable
    Identified: 10/07/1966
    Casualty Type: Non-hostile, died while missing
    Casualty Reason: Fixed Wing - Noncrew
    Casualty Detail: Air loss or crash over land
    URL: /VirtualWall.org/dl/LittsJG01a.htm
    Data accessed: 8/26/2020

THE VIRTUAL WALL ®   www.VirtualWall.org

Print This Page   Close This Page
Page template 10/09/2015

James Garris Litts

Private First Class
HHC, 8TH ENG BN, 1ST CAV DIV, USARV
Army of the United States
Bushkill, Pennsylvania
February 01, 1947 to October 04, 1966
JAMES G LITTS is on the Wall at Panel 11E, Line 45
See the full profile or name rubbing for James Litts

Henry Lee Creek

ON THE WALL: **Panel 11E Line 44**

This page Copyright© 1997-2018 www.VirtualWall.org Ltd.

PERSONAL DATA:

  Home of Record: Dallas, TX

  Date of birth: 12/04/1943

MILITARY DATA:

  Service Branch: Army of the United States

  Grade at loss: E3

  Rank: Private First Class

Promotion Note: None

  ID No: 54384182

  MOS: 11C10: Indirect Fire Infantryman

  Length Service: 00

  Unit: HHC, 1ST BN, 12TH CAVALRY, 1ST CAV
                     DIV, USARV

CASUALTY DATA:

  Start Tour: 07/23/1966

  Incident Date: 10/04/1966

  Casualty Date: 10/04/1966

  Status Date: Not Applicable

  Status Change: Not Applicable

  Age at Loss: 22

  Location: Binh Dinh Province, South Vietnam

  Remains: Body recovered

  Repatriated: Not Applicable

  Identified: 10/07/1966

  Casualty Type: Non-hostile, died while missing

  Casualty Reason: Fixed Wing - Noncrew

  Casualty Detail: Air loss or crash over land

  URL: /VirtualWall.org/dc/CreekHL01a.htm

  Data accessed: 10/1/2020

THE VIRTUAL WALL ®   www.VirtualWall.org

Print This Page   Close This Page

Page template 10/09/2015

Henry Lee Creek
Private First Class
HHC, 1ST BN, 12TH CAVALRY, 1ST CAV DIV, USARV
Army of the United States
Dallas, Texas
December 04, 1943 to October 04, 1966
HENRY L CREEK is on the Wall at Panel 11E, Line 44
See the full profile or name rubbing for Henry Creek

Ronald Eugene Lewis

ON THE WALL: **Panel 11E Line 45**

This page Copyright© 1997-2018 www.VirtualWall.org Ltd.

PERSONAL DATA:
  Home of Record: Chicago, IL
  Date of birth: 12/15/1943

MILITARY DATA:
  Service Branch: Army of the United States
  Grade at loss: E3
  Rank: Private First Class
Promotion Note: None
  ID No: 16831045
  MOS: 11B10: Infantryman
  Length Service: 01
  Unit: 2ND PLT, B CO, 1ST BN, 5TH CAVALRY,
                      1ST CAV DIV, USARV

CASUALTY DATA:
  Start Tour: 12/09/1965
  Incident Date: 10/04/1966
  Casualty Date: 10/04/1966
  Status Date: Not Applicable
  Status Change: Not Applicable
  Age at Loss: 22
  Location: Binh Dinh Province, South Vietnam
  Remains: Body recovered
  Repatriated: Not Applicable
  Identified: Not Applicable
  Casualty Type: Non-hostile, died while missing
  Casualty Reason: Fixed Wing - Noncrew
  Casualty Detail: Air loss or crash over land
  URL: /VirtualWall.org/dl/LewisRE03a.htm
  Data accessed: 8/26/2020

THE VIRTUAL WALL ®   www.VirtualWall.org

Print This Page   Close This Page
Page template 10/09/2015

Ronald Eugene Lewis

Private First Class
2ND PLT, B CO, 1ST BN, 5TH CAVALRY, 1ST CAV DIV, USARV
Army of the United States
Chicago, Illinois
December 15, 1943 to October 04, 1966
RONALD E LEWIS is on the Wall at Panel 11E, Line 45
See the full profile or name rubbing for Ronald Lewis

Donald Allen Smith Jr

ON THE WALL: **Panel 11E Line 47**

This page Copyright© 1997-2018 www.VirtualWall.org Ltd.

PERSONAL DATA:
  Home of Record: Royal Oak, MI
  Date of birth: 05/08/1946
MILITARY DATA:
  Service Branch: Army of the United States
  Grade at loss: E3
  Rank: Private First Class
Promotion Note: None
  ID No: 55829196
  MOS: 21B10: REDSTONE Electronic Mechanic
  Length Service: 00
  Unit: A CO, 5TH BN, 7TH CAVALRY, 1ST CAV
                     DIV, USARV
CASUALTY DATA:
  Start Tour: 08/02/1966
  Incident Date: 10/04/1966
  Casualty Date: 10/04/1966
  Status Date: Not Applicable
  Status Change: Not Applicable
  Age at Loss: 20
  Location: Binh Dinh Province, South Vietnam
  Remains: Body recovered
  Repatriated: Not Applicable
  Identified: Not Applicable
  Casualty Type: Non-hostile, died while missing
  Casualty Reason: Fixed Wing - Noncrew
  Casualty Detail: Air loss or crash over land
  URL: /VirtualWall.org/ds/SmithDA04a.htm
  Data accessed: 8/26/2020

THE VIRTUAL WALL ®   www.VirtualWall.org

Donald Allen Smith, Jr

Private First Class
A CO, 5TH BN, 7TH CAVALRY, 1ST CAV DIV, USARV
Army of the United States
Royal Oak, Michigan
May 08, 1946 to October 04, 1966
DONALD A SMITH Jr **is on the Wall at** Panel 11E, Line 47
See the full profile **or** name rubbing **for Donald Smith**

APPENDIX B
RIVER + MILL = TOWN

I HAVE A STRONG sense of place, and my roots have had a significant impact on my life. I lived the first eighteen years of my life in a dying mill town, Natick, along the banks of the Pawtuxet River in Rhode Island.

> When the glaciers that covered New England in the Ice Age receded, the melting ice cut numerous riverbeds along the four-hundred-foot decline from the northern and western borders of Rhode Island down into the Narragansett Bay. They also left numerous ponds, lakes, and coves amid the ridges and island peaks. The Blackstone River, the Moshassuck, the Woonasquatucket, and the Pawtuxet rivers were fast-moving, almost never frozen, and never dry. Their various falls and small ponds (for water storage behind dams) proved perfectly adapted for mill wheels to generate steady and certain sources of power.[16]

The sites along the Pawtuxet River that were "perfectly adapted for mill wheels" were soon recognized and readily adapted by early settlers. As the river flowed from its sources in Scituate and Coventry, dams and mills were built. Around each dam and mill, a small town was established that grew and prospered. The towns that grew around each mill are etched in my memory.

Along the southern branch of the Pawtuxet arose the mill towns of Washington, Anthony, Quidnick, Crompton, and Centerville. Along the northern branch were Hope, Jackson, Fiskville, Arkright,

Harris, Phenix (sic), and Lippitt. The two branches joined at River Point, which was the name of another mill and town, followed by Natick, Pontiac, and Hillsgrove before the river ends its journey into the Narragansett Bay.

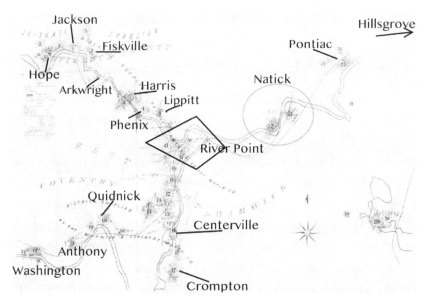

The mill towns along the Pawtuxet River

Each town is a living memory of times gone by, a virtual history of the Industrial Revolution. These towns hosted some of the earliest battles between management and labor along with the rise of fabulous fortunes and wealth amidst the poverty of company houses, stores, and farms. Today, they contain all the skeletal residue of the post-Industrial Era and the struggle of immigrant populations to survive and prosper, despite all their initial hardships.

The Pawtuxet River and the valley it carved on its way to the Narragansett Bay imprinted themselves forever in my mind and in my memory. After leaving my boyhood home over sixty-eight years ago, the river keeps coming back to me, and it grows larger each time I revisit it in my imagination.

During my life away from the Pawtuxet, as I matured and tasted different layers of life's experiences, my mind always takes me back to my boyhood home and neighborhood and the mill town of Natick on the Pawtuxet River. It seems I am compelled to go back in memory, as a sort of sanity check, to compare where I am now in life with the life I knew as a boy growing up along its banks.

FROM A BIRD'S-EYE VIEW

As my life progressed, my view of the river expanded as well. I began to see the river and its valley in my mind from progressively higher and higher levels of elevation. During my business travel days later in life, I had occasions to experience the ultimate bird's-eye view of the river and its valley while on home-bound flights. Toward the end of these long flights, I always had promise of relieving the tedium as the aircraft approached North America, knowing that the bird's-eye view was possible. On the flight progress screen in front of the cabin, I note that Delta 73 has made landfall near St. John's. Right on time—seven hours into the flight from Munich to John F. Kennedy Airport. With nearly 150 overseas trips, flight formats and timing had become very familiar to me.

The aircraft flies south along the coast from St. John's toward New York. Flying at 35,000 feet with clear visibility and good weather, I can easily spot the Cape Cod hook and the greater Boston area. However, it's the terrain just south of this area that really excites me. Sometimes the airplane flies along the coast, and I have a bird's-eye view of the entire state of Rhode Island, looking north toward Providence with the Jamestown and Newport Bridges spanning the Narragansett Bay in the foreground. I can just make out the bend in the bay that forms Warwick Neck, and tucked behind it is the Pawtuxet River Valley and the little mill town of Natick where I was born.

On other flights, the airplanes fly directly over Providence and south toward Westerly along the west side of the Narragansett Bay.

On these flights, I am able to look down and identify Warwick Cove, Francis T. Greene Airport, the Old Post Road (Route 1) and Interstate 95 as it winds its way north-south through Rhode Island. Although it is difficult, I always feel I can identify the Pawtuxet River Valley as it flows east toward the Narragansett Bay, and I can measure in my mind where Natick and my old neighborhood should be. Thoughts of my sister, Theresa, and brother, Mike—still living there—and my parents, buried together in a grave some six miles below me, always make me very nostalgic.

I am aware of the land slipping beneath me at 500 miles per hour. In just twenty minutes, the jetliner will be landing at John F. Kennedy Airport. I recall that it takes about three hours to drive the same distance on Interstate 95 to New York City from where I lived in Rhode Island.

I never cease to marvel at each ocean crossing. My business trips took me to London, Paris, Munich, and occasionally the Middle East, and I begin to think about the immigrants and their travel to the United States from these parts of the world. My parents and grandparents had been part of that wave of immigrants coming to the United States in the late nineteenth century. From cushy frequent-flyer upgrades, I eat caviar and drink champagne as I cross the ocean. I can only begin to imagine the hardships of travel just one hundred years ago.

Within minutes, the Boeing 767 swings out over the Atlantic and circles Sandy Hook in a holding pattern before landing. As it makes its final approach to JFK, I can see the Statue of Liberty and Ellis Island off to the left in New York Harbor. I remember that at eleven months old, my mother had arrived in the United States on one of the early liners crammed with Italian immigrants. I can imagine her being held by my grandmother as they passed the Statue of Liberty on their way to Ellis Island.

APPENDIX C
MILITARY NOTES

ARMY BLUE, TRADITIONAL TUNE played for "Graduating Class Front and Center, March," when the First Class steps out of ranks for the final time as cadets, and also played for the last dance at all hops, has its beginning as the song of the Class of 1865. The first six stanzas were written by L.W. Becklaw, and the tune is that of an old minstrel song, *Aura Lea*. As years passed innumerable verses were added to this, and only a few of the more renowned can be presented. The allusion to the "cup" has reference to the "class baby cup" which was to be presented to the parents of the first male child of the class. "Old plebe camp" has disappeared in the passing of Camp Clinton, once the scene of summer training. (From the 1947 *Bugle Notes*.)

Army Blue

We've not much longer here to stay,
For in a month or two,
We'll bid farewell to "Kaydet Grey,"
And don the "Army Blue."
Chorus:
Army Blue, Army Blue,
Hurrah for the Army Blue,
We'll bid farewell to "Kaydet Grey,"
And don the "Army Blue."
With pipe and song we'll jog along.
Till this short time is through,

And all among our jovial throng,

Have donned the Army Blue.

Chorus.

To the ladies who come up in June,

We'll bid a fond adieu,

Here's hoping they be married soon,

And join the Army too.

Chorus.

'Twas the song we sang in old plebe camp,

When first our grey was new,

The song we sang on summer nights,

That song of Army Blue.

Chorus.

Now, fellows, we must say goodbye,

We've stuck our four years thru,

Our future is a cloudless sky,

We'll don the Army Blue.

Chorus.

Then and now, from my West Point Class of 1957 50th Anniversary Yearbook:

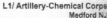

Joseph Raymond (Joe) Tedeschi Sue

L1/ Artillery-Chemical Corps Medford N.J

When I walked through that sally port, I knew so little about West Point and even less about the Army. Nothing in my RI upbringing pointed me in this direction. It launched a whole new world for me. The true love of my life, Sue Oebbecke, "joined the Army too" on 20 July 1957. Both our daughters were born Army Brats, Susanne (HI) and Marly (Aberdeen). Career favorites: Army sponsored advanced schooling at IA State, exchange officer with British Army at their Defence NBC School, several Washington/Pentagon assignments, commander/director of the Foreign Science and Technology Center in Charlottesville.

In Viet Nam 1966, I experienced one of those life-altering events: I survived as a passenger when the Caribou aircraft flew into the side of Hong Kong Mountain at An Khe. Over the years, I've learned to describe this experience in a short hand way: Every day is Christmas!

I began a second career for 14 years with General Electric/Martin Marietta/Lockheed Martin - same job, different bosses. Program manager for the Counter Battery Radar (COBRA), I lived this program from its concept, sold it as a package to the governments of France, Germany and United Kingdom, retiring in 1999 after the first three prototypes were built. A very satisfying experience. Latest venture occurred when I entered the diaconate program in the Diocese of Trenton just prior to my second retirement, and was ordained a deacon in 2002. It's been 26 moves since I walked through that sally port, but life seems to have settled down now around Medford, St. Mary of the Lakes Parish, our condo in Brigantine, our daughters and their great husbands, and our five wonderful grandchildren. Every day is Christmas!

My life in a nutshell

CHRONOLOGY OF ARMY CAREER ASSIGNMENTS
COL. JOSEPH R. TEDESCHI
(RET.)

Years	Grade / Rank	Assignment
1957	O-1 Second Lieutenant	Graduated, United States Military Academy, West Point, New York Student, Officer Basic Course, US Army Field Artillery School, Ft. Sill, Oklahoma.
1958–59	O-2 First Lieutenant	Forward Observer, Mortar Battery, 14th Inf, 25th Inf Div, Hawaii. Became thoroughly familiar with 4.2-inch mortar operations and weapon characteristics.
1960–61	O-2 First Lieutenant	Assistant Division Chemical Officer, 25th Inf Div, Hawaii. Performed staff functions involving division wide training and readiness for combat operations.
1961–63	O-3 Captain	Army-sponsored, full-time graduate student, Iowa State University, Ames, Iowa. Master of Science degree.

Years	Grade / Rank	Assignment
1963–65	O-3 Captain	Research and Development Coordinator, US Army Test and Evaluation Command, Aberdeen Proving Ground, Maryland. Completed successful operational and service tests of XM 454 Nuclear Projectile. Also responsible for operational and service tests of all Army developed Prescribed Action Link (PAL) devices for nuclear weapons and radiological detection (RADIAC) instruments.
1965–66	O-3 Captain	Student, Chemical Officer Advanced Course, US Army Chemical Center and School, Ft. McClellan, Alabama. Received thorough grounding in full range of Nuclear, Biological, and Chemical (NBC) subjects and combat operations.
1966	O-4 Major	Division Chemical Officer, 1st Air Cav Div, Vietnam. Injured in air accident and medevaced to Continental US.
1967–69	O-4 Major	Research and Development Coordinator, HQ, US Army Materiel Command, Washington, DC. Contributed significantly to R&D programs of materiel being developed for use in Vietnam.

Years	Grade / Rank	Assignment
1969–70	O-4 Major	Student, US Army Command and General Staff College, Ft. Leavenworth, Kansas. Received mid-level professional development schooling on combined arms operations at the division, corps, and army levels.
1970–72	O-5 Lieutenant Colonel	US Army Exchange Officer, British Defense NBC School, Salisbury, United Kingdom. Instructed on US Army NBC operations for British Forces Officer and NCO courses. Also, Chief of Trials Division conducting hands-on service trials of full range of UK NBC equipment.
1972–73	O-5 Lieutenant Colonel	Battalion Commander, School Battalion, US Army Chemical Center and School, Ft. McClellan, Alabama. Commanded 800-man battalion providing total support to Chemical School. Conducted field exercises in support of Chemical School's training mission. Battalion Commander, 2nd Chemical Battalion until deactivation in 1973.

Years	Grade / Rank	Assignment
1974	O-5 Lieutenant Colonel	Staff Officer, US Army Military Personnel Center, Washington, DC. Eight months' experience in officer assignments, development of personnel policies, selection criteria for promotion, advanced schooling and professional development. Interim duty for one month to command Mobile Training Team in Iran to conduct NBC training for Iranian Army. Provided training and briefings at highest level of Iranian Armed Forces Command and Staff.
1974–75	O-5 Lieutenant Colonel	Student, Industrial College of the Armed Forces, Ft. McNair, Washington, DC. Highest level professional military development and training in the assessment and planning for mobilization of the national industrial base to support the national defense effort.

Years	Grade / Rank	Assignment
1975–77	O-6 Colonel	Executive Officer, Systems Review and Analysis Office, Office of Deputy Chief of Staff for Research, Development and Acquisition (ODCSRDA), Department of Army (DA) Staff, Washington, DC. Principal duty as Executive Secretary to Army System Acquisition Review Council (ASARC). Insured detailed preparation was accomplished for meetings of ASARC, the highest level, DA decision-making body on materiel acquisition. Conducted 22 ASARC meetings in two-year period during which critical milestone decisions were made on such systems as the M-1 Tank, AAH and Blackhawk helicopters, and the AN/TPQ-36 and 37 Mortar and Artillery Locating Radars.

Years	Grade / Rank	Assignment
1977–79	O-6 Colonel	Chief, Support Systems Division, Combat Support Directorate, ODCSRDA, DA, Washington, DC. Supervised a twenty-nine person staff responsible for preparing a wide range of programs for research, development and procurement of Army support systems (e.g., trucks). Involved total planning, programming, and budgeting for multi-million-dollar systems for two complete fiscal years. Proposed and defended programs at highest management levels at DA, DoD and Congressional Budget Staffs.
1979–81	O-6 Colonel	Executive Officer, Research, Development and Acquisition Directorate, HQ, US Army Development and Readiness Command (DARCOM), Washington, DC. Intimately involved at front office level in the total RDA process (planning, programming, budgeting, execution, and review) at the highest-level Army field command responsible for these functions. Scope of effort covered the total Army materiel program.

Years	Grade / Rank	Assignment
1981–84	O-6 Colonel	Commander/Director, US Army Foreign Science and Technology Center, Charlottesville, Virginia. Commanded and directed a multi-disciplined, 560 person, $26M annual budget, all-source, worldwide, scientific and technical intelligence organization to meet the requirements of the US Army DARCOM, the Assistant Chief of Staff for Intelligence, DA, and the Defense Intelligence Agency.
1984	O-6 Colonel	Chief, Maritime/United Nations Division, Organization of the Joint Chiefs of Staff, Washington, DC. Responsible for coordinating Joint Staff positions on all ongoing arms control and disarmament negotiations at the Conference on Disarmament in Geneva and the First Committee, UN, New York.

OLDEST GRAD SPEECH
FOUNDER'S DAY DINNER
UNION LEAGUE
13 MARCH 2009

THANK YOU, MR. PRESIDENT (Michael Parrish),

General Hagenbeck, Distinguished Guests, Fellow Graduates,

I'd like to give you this old grad's perspective on West Point looking back fifty-two years by using a couple of West Point stories as my crutch—one of them on the light side and one more serious. To tee up the first story, I want to tell you why I really accepted the honor to give the "old grad" speech this year. I accepted this honor because now, now, I finally have the chance to tell a very personal, up-front story, and it involves General Alexander M. Haig, Jr., the illustrious graduate of our alma mater, whose storied accomplishments have been recognized by our West Point Society of Philadelphia with the prestigious annual Guardian of Liberty Award which bears his name.

I'm certain you all know that General Haig was the US Secretary of State in 1981–1982 and the Supreme Allied Commander, Europe, from 1974–1979. It's common knowledge that General Haig was the White House Chief of Staff in 1973–74 and the VCSA (Vice Chief of Staff of the Army) in 1973, but how many of you know that General Haig was the Company M-1 Tac Officer in 1953! Well, my story takes place in the fall of 1953, a Saturday morning in ranks inspection—one of my first as a plebe.

We did the open ranks thing, and in time, Major Alexander Haig and the cadet platoon leader, with pen and quill pad in hand, made their way down the ranks toward me. Now, I had prepared very hard for this inspection, and I thought I was really ready—brass, shoes, belts, haircut, rifle, the whole works. Major Alexander Haig did a left face and pivoted in front of me. My heart was pounding as I came to inspection arms and slid the bolt of my M-1 rifle open. Major Haig was very old school, and he gave me the top-of-the-head to the tip-of-the-toe thorough inspection, and I thought I had nailed it when he returned my rifle to me. I waited anxiously for him to pivot and move to the victim next to me. Instead, he turned to the cadet platoon leader and said, "This man is out of uniform. He has his cuff links on backwards. Let's do a better job of teaching these plebes how to wear the cadet uniform."

And there you have it! My moment of fame, which I share with you. How many of you grads can claim to have been gigged by General Haig for wearing his cuff links backwards? Well, I can. That's my story, and I'm sticking to it!

My second story concerns class rings and our cherished motto "Duty, Honor, Country." I'll be brief about setting this one up. The time was October 1966, and the place was the Clark Air Force Base [AFB] hospital in the Philippines. A week before, I had been in an airplane crash in Vietnam—the C-7 Caribou, in which I was flying as a passenger along with thirty-two other people, flew into the side of Hon Cong Mountain near An Khe during a blinding fog.

I was one of the fortunate survivors; I survived the crash with a broken hip and was being medevaced through channels with the first stop out of Vietnam being Clark AFB.

I had been placed in a spica body cast to immobilize me, and I relate this story from the perspective of being in that full, rigid, horizontal body cast, completely dependent on others for just about everything. I attempted to recall years later as much of what happened when we arrived at Clark in a short piece I wrote for our class's 50th Anniversary Year Book, part of which was to collect the Vietnam experiences of our class. I would like to read this excerpt from that piece to you:

[Here I repeat my story from pages 101–104 about meeting Kitsy Westmoreland upon arrival at Clark Air Force Base.]

Kitsy Westmoreland's actions were clearly much more than a token or symbolic gesture by the wife of the senior US military officer in Vietnam. This was very hard work that filled a real need in providing comfort and relief to immobilized wounded and injured military men coming out of Vietnam. No—this was the act of a very classy lady who matched her feelings and beliefs with actions and example. I doubt that most of the men she bathed and comforted ever knew her name or who she really was.

That ends the excerpt from my little written piece—and my story about Kitsy Westmoreland, a member of our West Point family. This story will not be found in the *New York Times* or the *Washington Post*, not in 1966 and not today. This story, however, is very important to me, and I wanted to share it with you, because it says everything I want to say to you about Duty, Honor, and Country—the motto engraved on the sides of our class rings—and how Kitsy Westmoreland lived it. Which leads me to some final thoughts on West Point.

From this old grad's perspective looking back fifty-two years, I tend to remember and cherish two things about West Point: first, the physical place, and second—always, always—the wonderful West Point stories.

As for the physical place and the changes made at West Point since my time, they are most welcome. None of this "the Corps has" for this old grad! I commend General Hagenbeck and all the Supes [superintendents] over the years who have fought for and made changes to the stone and brick and mortar at West Point. West Point will continue to physically change, and it will never be exactly the same way you remembered it.

So, in the long run, all we have left to cherish, really, are the stories. And it's the stories that will stick with you, just like the two stories I've told tonight that have become part of my life. It's the stories that end up really defining West Point and who we are as West Point graduates.

And toward that end, I seriously commend to you a wonderful source, a wellspring of West Point stories to inspire you and amaze you and touch you. I'm referring to the Taps Supplement and the *Assembly* magazine which contains the life stories of our beloved departed comrades. In my heart, I know it will be these incredible, amazing, wonderfully completed stories that will endure long after the brick and mortar have crumbled—and West Point will forever be proclaimed by them.

Thank you for honoring me as the oldest grad and giving me the privilege of sharing with you two of *my* West Point stories. BEAT NAVY!

APPENDIX D
SUPPORTING MATERIAL

NEWLYWEDS
Near the
Front Lines

In Vietnam, this husband-wife Army nurse
team lives within enemy mortar range
and works around-the-clock to save lives

Photos and Text By ROBERT J. ELLISON

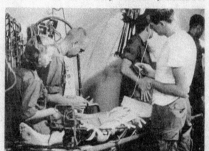

Above, the Williamses—Mr. and Mrs. Army Nurse—attend wounded GI at An Khe. They are on 24-hour call.

When off duty (left), they live in "hootch" Bob built himself. They're talking to Nick, a hospital "mascot."

Their first home (below) is unsightly and crowded, yet they may extend tour. Barb misses most cooking meals.

BARBARA WILLIAMS, a bride of three months, got a call from her husband Bob. It was a message many young wives are getting these days.

"I'm going to Vietnam," Bob said.

"No kidding!" Barbara exclaimed. After a pause, she added, "Well, then so am I."

Three months after Bob landed in Vietnam, Barbara joined him. They started setting up their first "real home"—a tent within mortar range of the Viet Cong.

Bob and Barbara are both Army medical-surgical nurses, two of the more than 600 nurses who take care of our fighting men in Vietnam (an estimated 500 of the nurses are women). The Williamses, 1st lieutenants, met while studying nursing at Columbus (Ohio) State Hospital.

They are stationed at An Khe in the high lands, home of the 1st Cavalry Division. Since arriving there last year, Bob has scrounged material to build a "hootch" (GI terminology for housing) with tin walls and roof, concrete-slab floor, and a true luxury—one glass window. They spend little time there, however, because their 2nd Surgical Hospital handles most of the 1st Cav's casualties and they are on 24-hour call.

Recreation consists only of movies and softball games, but life isn't dull. All night copters churn over their hootch, bringing in casualties, and in the distance artillery booms. "But the mosquitoes almost make as much noise as both," Bob says.

The VC have mounted one mortar attack against the hospital, and periodically the Williamses, donning flak jackets and steel helmets, are routed out of bed.

How do they enjoy newlywed life in a war zone? Their first tour of duty is ending. "We're thinking of extending another six months," Bob says. "We couldn't pull out of here if we're still needed." ✦

*Husband and Wife Nurse Team – Poughkeepsie Journal
(June 18, 1967)*

VIETNAM VET COUPLE DEAD IN AIR CRASH

CINCINNATI (AP) — The first husband-wife nurse team to serve in the Vietnam war died in a plane crash here yesterday.

Authorities said the plane apparently exploded after takeoff, killing Robert A. Williams, 37, his wife Barbara, 29, and their two-month-old son Jeffrey. They lived in Floydad, Tex. He was a hospital administrator.

The couple attracted national attention in 1966 as a married team serving in a combat zone.

Based near An Khe in Vietnam's Central Highlands, they were attached to the Second Surgical Hospital of the 1st Air Cavalry Division.

The plane accident occurred as they left for Texas from a holiday visit with Mrs. Williams' parents.

Witnesses said the plane made a screaming noise and broke apart moments after takeoff It crashed in the wooded backyard of a home near the Blue Ash Airport, in suburban Cincinnati.

The sad news Bob Ray sent me with the previous article about the husband and wife nurse team

MISSED APPROACH

... the CV-2 was approaching from the southeast at a low altitude.
The landing gear was down and the aircraft was heading toward the mountain.

GCA controller: "A Caribou was calling approach control on a common frequency, so I was receiving the call the same as approach control. They were having a little bit of trouble locating him, so I offered my assistance because they didn't have SIF/IFF interrogator equipment and we did. I located it after I had the pilot squawk for identification. I got positive radar contact seven miles south. The Caribou was proceeding on a southwesterly heading.

"I saw that in approximately two miles it would intercept the on-course. I advised approach control that I had a weak target on it and a strong IFF return. I asked if they had any contact on radar, but I got the impression they were too busy at the time. They tried to find him, but they were working a departure at the same time. As the Caribou crossed the on-course, I decided I'd take control of the aircraft and give the pilot a right turn.

"I zeroed his turn, gave him the lost communication procedure and all runway information for a surveillance approach to runway 34. He acknowledged all transmissions. . . . I rolled him out on final and he appeared to roll out on course at approximately eight and one-half miles, heading 345°. At this point, I lost radar contact. All I had was the IFF. I advised the pilot that I had lost radar contact and had an IFF target only, and that the continuation of the approach would be IFF target, with no radar separation applied. He acknowledged and I noticed the IFF target to be slightly left of the on-course. . . .

"I saw a video target once again at approximately seven and one-half miles. It appeared to be left of the on-course, maybe a quarter of a mile. The

IFF target appeared to be very close to on-course, maybe slightly left. At this time, I gave the pilot a right turn to 040°. I wanted to see how he tracked as long as I had video. I wanted to give him a considerable turn so I could figure out a good heading for final. However, I lost radar contact again and was still on IFF. I brought him back on course and rolled him out with a heading of 350°, this time at seven miles. . . . I told him to prepare to begin his descent in one mile. I gave him another check, a 15-second warning to begin his descent in 15 seconds at six miles. I told him to begin his descent from 4,500 and that GCA recommended 750 fpm for 90 knots. This was the second time I advised him of this. I always advise an aircraft a second time so the pilot gets it for sure. . . . I told him not to acknowledge further transmissions on final unless requested to do so.

". . . At five miles, I gave him a passing altitude of 4,000 feet. He advised me that he was at 4,300 feet and making up for it. At this time, I gave him slightly left of course. . . . He proceeded inbound and at four miles I gave him a slight left correction . . . then on course, and told him his passing altitude should be 3,500 feet in his descent. He acknowledged, saying 'We've made up for it,' meaning that he had made up for his higher altitude at the five mile mark.

"At that time, my IFF target started to bloom. I got a bulging target. . . . I was still trying to get a video return from the aircraft, but was unable to at three miles. I gave him no on-course information at three miles because I wasn't sure of it. The target was blooming badly left and right at that time. I told the pilot that his passing altitude

should be 3,000 feet in his descent and he acknowledged. . . . I was concerned over the blooming target, so I decided to call the approach off just out of
3,000 feet and three miles. I told the pilot radar
contact was lost and to execute a missed approach,
climbing outbound on a heading of 360° to 3,500
feet. I told him to reverse his course with a left
turn when he reached 3,500 feet, and to contact
approach control. The pilot acknowledged. Approximately 20 seconds later, I got another transmission from him asking the frequency to contact
approach control. I gave him the frequency and he
said, 'Thank you.' That was the last transmission
I got from him. . . ."

Question: "After you got identification of this
aircraft, you vectored it to a position where you
could put it on final approach. Is this true?"

Answer: "Partially. It crossed the on-course while
approach control was trying to get a target on it.
I had to reverse the pilot's course and descend him
to an altitude to intercept the glide path."

Question: "Do you know what his altitude was
when he started descending?"

Answer: "I'm pretty sure that it was 5,500 feet.
I gave the pilot a right turn to a heading of 090°,
and instructed him to descend to and maintain
4,500 feet."

Question: "Did he acknowledge this when you
gave it to him?"

Answer: "Yes, he did."

Question: "You indicated that when you did
this you had a weak radar target and a strong IFF
return. Would you explain this?"

Answer: "Yes. The radar was working at half
power that day and from what I can understand

. . . the pilots did not have a full understanding of the implications of an IFF only approach. They did not realize that their position in relationship to the centerline could not be accurately pinpointed.

from conversations with previous pilots we had given departures to, the overcast was quite heavy. At half power, it's difficult for the radar to cut through the overcast. It is actually quite a job when operating at full power. The IFF return is not the same. I was getting a strong IFF return and a weak radar return."

Question: "What type of advisory did you give the pilot at that time?"

Answer: "I advised him that the continuation of his approach would be with an IFF target only and that radar separation could not be applied."

Question: "What was his answer to your advisory?"

Answer: "I don't remember his exact words. It was something like 'wonderful' or 'marvelous.' It gave me the indication that he wasn't too excited about getting an IFF approach, but did approve of it."

Question: "What were your intentions by continuing the IFF? Did you hope to get radar back and bring him in, or were you attempting to vector him to the airfield?"

Answer: "My intention was to give him an approach using IFF. When the IFF started getting out of hand, I realized the approach could not be continued and I discontinued it by giving him a missed approach."

Witness: "Another soldier and I noticed a CV-2 approaching from the southeast at a low altitude.

The landing gear was down and the aircraft was heading toward the mountain. The top of the mountain was completely hidden by fog. As the aircraft approached our position, there was no change in the pitch of the engines, and none as it neared the mountain. As the aircraft disappeared into the fog, we heard the sound of an apparent crash."

The airplane struck trees, crashed, and came to rest inverted. The crew of four and nine passengers were killed. Two passengers sustained critical injuries, 14 passengers sustained major injuries, and three passengers escaped with minor injuries.

The point at which the Caribou struck the mountain was measured and determined to be 4,300 feet left of the approach path for runway 34.

Investigation board analysis: ". . . Sensing that approach control was busy assisting an aircraft which was outbound, and apparently unable to concentrate on a target for the approaching aircraft, the controller decided to direct the surveillance approach. After transmitting adjustment turns, the control targeted the aircraft as on-course, eight and one-half nautical miles from touchdown. The controller transmitted missed approach instructions which were acknowledged by the pilots. The controller stated that the GCA equipment was presenting a weak radar target and a strong IFF interrogator return. He again stated that at the eight and one-half nautical mile mark, he lost radar

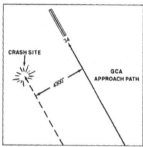

contact and had only IFF interrogator return. At this point, the GCA controller advised the pilots that radar contact had been lost and that he was receiving an IFF target only. He further transmitted that the continuation of the approach would be with an IFF target and no radar separation could be applied. This condition was acknowledged by the pilots.

"After discussions with other pilots, and analysis by the board members, it is the opinion of the board that the pilots did not have a full understanding of the implications of an IFF only approach. They did not realize that their position in relation to the centerline could not be accurately pinpointed. When a duplicate approach was made, operating the GCA equipment at one-half power, the radar video target was lost prior to the time the aircraft was established on the final approach course. The operator was unable to regain the radar video target. During this duplicating approach, the weather conditions, with the exception of precipitation, were such that the aircraft had to be targeted while flying through clouds. Although the cloud conditions were not a duplicate of those present at the time of the crash, the GCA equipment was required to target the aircraft while it was in clouds. . . .

"The IFF interrogator target return presents an arc shaped target which can cover as much as a two-mile area on the radar scope. During a sur-

veillance approach, the GCA controllers, under normal conditions, provide course and distance information. Altitude is the responsibility of the pilot. Advisory service for altitude at various distance marks is furnished by the GCA controller. Altitude advisories were given to the pilots of the crashed aircraft at each mile interval. . . . "

Indorsements: "Concur with the finding that the descent of the aircraft to 2,100 feet after issuance and receipt of missed approach instructions constitutes the primary cause of the accident. Likewise, concur that a principal contributing cause was the use of the SIF/IFF interrogator beacon, with resultant inaccuracy. . . ."

"Notwithstanding improvement in ground navigational equipment and controller personnel, it remains the fundamental responsibility of the aviators to comply with emergency instructions as issued."

"There was one additional navigational instrument available and evidently functioning which, if used, would have indicated to the pilot that he was considerably to the left of the approach course. This was the ADF which was tuned to the ADF beacon at the airfield, but evidently not used as a crosscheck by the pilot or copilot.

"Failure to use all available instruments as crosschecks during instrument approaches is a habit easily acquired and constant emphasis on avoiding this habit is essential."

APPENDIX E
THE RAY FAMILY

Bob Ray's early and late career photos

BOB RAY'S OBITUARY

Colonel Robert Luman Ray, US Army, Ret.

Col. Robert L. Ray, Ret., former resident of Annandale, VA, died July 22, 2013, after a 25-year battle with Parkinson's disease.

Col. Ray, 78, was born December 20, 1934, in Brooklyn, NY, the only child of Russell Luman Ray, a newspaper correspondent for the Brooklyn Eagle, and Rose Eleanor Pullich, a school principal in Brooklyn, who also served as a Democratic district leader in New York.

Col. Ray graduated from Brooklyn Prep in 1952 and from St. Lawrence University in 1956, where he was an ROTC distinguished military cadet and regimental commander. He received his MA in Administration from George Washington University in 1965. He attended the US Army Command and General Staff College in 1966 and the US Army War College in 1973.

Col. Ray was a highly decorated career soldier who retired in 1986 after 30 years of military service. He served two tours of duty in Vietnam. In October of 1966, he was one of only a few survivors of a military plane crash in An Khe, Vietnam. Following a four-month recovery in the hospital in Japan, he returned directly to combat in Vietnam to complete his first tour of duty. His military career included command assignments in Vietnam (1966–67; 1970–71), Turkey (1977–78), Germany (1958–61; 1979–81) and Korea (1982–85). His military honors include the Legion of Merit and the Bronze Star, both with oak leaf clusters.

Col. Ray loved sports and the outdoors, enjoying fishing and hiking with his family at his boyhood vacation home in Mt. Beacon, NY. He was an avid Washington Redskins, New York Knicks and Brooklyn Dodgers fan. Most of all, he will be remembered as a devoted husband and father who was always there with unwavering love and support for his family.

He is survived by his beloved wife of 55 years, Margaret Bangs, whom he met when they were both teenagers. Together they were an inspiration to all who knew them.

Col. Ray is also survived by his three children, Robert, Russell (Elizabeth) and Roseann (Jeffrey), and his seven grandchildren, Caroline, William, Edward, Matthew, Andrew, Julia, and John.

A memorial service will be held at 8:45 a.m., Friday, September 13 at Memorial Chapel, Ft. Myer, VA. Col. Ray will be buried with full military honors at Arlington National Cemetery immediately following the service.

In lieu of flowers, Col. Ray would be honored to make a difference in the lives of disabled soldiers and their families who have sacrificed so much for their nation. Donations can be made to Vail Veterans.

Bob Ray and his children camping before his VN deployment, Rosann, Russell, and Bobby.

OBITUARY FOR PEGGY RAY

Obituary for Margaret Ann Ray (nee Bangs) (Age 81)

A former resident of Annandale, VA, died October 20, 2016, at the Sunrise at Mount Vernon after a long battle with Alzheimer's.

Peggy was born March 2, 1935, in Brooklyn, NY to William C. Bangs and Margaret (Crowe) Bangs.

She graduated valedictorian from Fontbonne Hall Academy in Brooklyn in 1953 and remained close with her classmates throughout her life. She married her high school sweetheart, Col. Robert Luman Ray, in 1958, and graduated cum laude from Fordham University in 1959 with a B.S. in Mathematics.

Peggy was most proud of being a soldier's wife and a loving mother. She enjoyed traveling the world, reading, and dancing with her husband. She was fiercely independent, kind-hearted, and a woman of deep faith. She will be remembered by her family and friends as a devoted wife who faced her husband's and her own medical challenges with an indomitable spirit and irrepressible optimism. Peggy and Bob were an inspiration to all who knew them. Peggy was preceded in death by her husband of 55 years. She is survived by her three children, Robert Ray, Russell (Elizabeth) Ray and Roseann (Jeffrey) Coyner; her seven grandchildren, Caroline, William, Edward, Matthew, Andrew, Julia, and John; three great-grandchildren, Luman, Grace, and Leo; her sister, Patricia Van Roten (Frank); and niece and nephews, Kara, Todd, and Peter.

A Funeral Mass will be held at 2:45 p.m. Monday, January 30 at the Old Post Chapel, Fort Myer, Virginia, followed by her burial next to her beloved husband at Arlington National Cemetery. A reception will be held at the Officers' Club at Fort Myer.

Peggy had spent a few years as a Carmelite Nun and has remained close to her Sisters throughout her life. In lieu of flowers, memorials may be made in Peggy's name to The Carmelite Monastery, 89 Hiddenbrooke Dr., Beacon, NY 12508 or to a charity of one's choice.[17]

Col. Bob Ray's grandson William C. Ray, son of attorney and former Whitewater Independent Council Robert W. Ray, carries on the military tradition of the family today. Bob and Peggy attended William Ray's graduation from the U.S. Air Force Academy in 2010, Bob's last air travel before he died. That grandson is now a major in the U.S. Space Force, currently serving with the space command in Denver, Colorado.

ENDNOTES

1. C. A. Swenson and J. R. Tedeschi, "Phase Transitions in Ammonium Fluoride," *Journal of Chemistry and Physics* 40 (1964):1141, https://doi.org/10.1063/1.1725262.

2. The Johnson-McConnell agreement of 1966 was an agreement between United States Army Chief of Staff General Harold K. Johnson and United States Air Force Chief of Staff General John P. McConnell on 6 April 1966. The US Army agreed to give up its fixed-wing tactical airlift aircraft, while the US Air Force relinquished its claim to most forms of rotary wing aircraft. The most immediate effect was the transfer of DHC-4 Caribou aircraft from the Army to the Air Force, the designation changing from the Army CV-2A and CV-2B to the Air Force C7-A and C7-B.

3. *M*A*S*H* was a TV show from 1972–1983 about a Mobile Army Surgical Hospital during the Korean War. This hospital was the 2nd Surgical Hospital (Army Mobile) which was a MASH.

4. From 1965 to 1973, the Bell UH-1, officially named "Iroquois" was the most common utility helicopter used in Vietnam. The "Huey" nickname stuck thanks to her early "HU-1" designation. It was later redesignated to UH-1 with the normalization of 1962.

5. Claude D. Newby, *It Took Heroes: A Calvary Chaplain's Memoir of Vietnam* (New York: Presidio Press, 2003), 31.

6. "Kitsy Westmoreland on Service, Family, and the Army Life," The West Point Center for Oral History, https://www.westpointcoh.org/interviews/kitsy-westmoreland-on-service-family-and-

the-army-life#:~:text=William%20Westmoreland%20died%20
in%202005%2C%20but%20Kitsy%20Westmoreland,Mamie%20-
Eisenhower%20and%20Dolores%20Hope%2C%20Bob%20
Hope's%20wife.

7. Robert W. Ray, a former federal prosecutor, served as the successor to Ken Starr as Independent Counsel in the Whitewater and Monica Lewinsky investigations. He also was part of then President Donald J. Trump's first impeachment defense team during his January 2020 trial before the United States Senate. Mr. Ray ("Bobby") is the son of Colonel Bob Ray who survived the plane crash with the author.

8. "De Havilland Canada DHC-4 Caribou," Virtual Aircraft Museum, http://www.aviastar.org/air/canada/dehavilland_caribou. php?p=1#cmt.

9. U.S. Army Otter-Caribou Association, http://www.otter-caribou. org.

10. The C-7A Caribou Association, http://www.c-7acaribou.com.

11. "Plane Crash on Hon Cong Mountain, 10/66," Vietnam War / An Khe / Hon Cong Mountain, https://jim4jet.webs.com/c7acaribou. htm.

12. Jake Hargis, "An Khe Caribou Crash," *C-7A Caribou Association* (June 2001): 8, http://www.c-7acaribou.com/news/v01i13.pdf.

13. "Vietnam War/An Khe/Hon Cong Mountain," https://jim4jet.webs. com/cariboucrashphotos.htm.

14. "De Havilland Canada," http://www.aviastar.orglair/ canadaldehavilland_caribou.php.

15. "Air Gas Station Saves 7 Jets," *The Miami Herald*, July 10, 1964, 78.

16. William G. McLoughlin, *Rhode Island, A History*, 115–16 (W.W. Norton & Co., 1978).

17. "Margaret Ann Ray," Obituaries, *The Washington Post*, Jan. 22, 2017. http://www.legacy.com/obituaries/washingtonpost/obituary.aspx?n=MARGARETRAY&pid=183677170#sthash.hwckSaVv.dpuf.